Soul of Christ

Soul of Christ

Meditations on a Timeless Prayer

Marie Paul Curley, FSP

BOOKS & MEDIA
Boston

Library of Congress Cataloging-in-Publication Data

Curley, Marie Paul.
  Soul of Christ : meditations on a timeless prayer / Marie Paul Curley, FSP.
    pages cm
  ISBN 978-0-8198-9030-6 -- ISBN 0-8198-9030-8
  I. Soul of Christ--Meditations. I. Title.
  BX2175.A5C87 2014
  242'.7--dc23

                          2014004611

The Scripture quotations contained herein are from the *New Revised Standard Version Bible: Catholic Edition,* copyright © 1989, 1993, Division of Christian Education of the National Council of the Churches of Christ in the United States of America. Used by permission. All rights reserved.

Cover design by Danielle Lussier

Cover photo by Danielle Lussier; back cover: Mary Emmanuel Alves, FSP

Published by Pauline Books & Media, 50 Saint Pauls Avenue, Boston, MA 02130-3491

Printed in the U.S.A.

www.pauline.org

Pauline Books & Media is the publishing house of the Daughters of St. Paul, an international congregation of women religious serving the Church with the communications media.

1 2 3 4 5 6 7 8 9   18 17 16 15 14

To my mother,
Mary Teresa Curley,
who first shared with me the *Anima Christi* prayer,
instilled in me a love for the Eucharist,
and started me off on the path of faith.

Mom,
thank you for the countless ways
you have loved me,
encouraged me,
and filled my life with joy.
Without you,
this book would not have been written.

Contents

Soul of Christ

(Anima Christi)

Soul of Christ, sanctify me.	*Anima Christi, sanctifica me.*
Body of Christ, save me.	*Corpus Christi, salva me.*
Blood of Christ, inebriate me.	*Sanguis Christi, inebria me.*
Water from the side of Christ, wash me.	*Aqua lateris Christi, lava me.*
Passion of Christ, strengthen me.	*Passio Christi, conforta me.*
O Good Jesus, hear me.	*O bone Iesu, exaudi me.*
Within Your wounds hide me.	*Intra tua vulnera absconde me.*
Permit me not to be separated from You.	*Ne permittas me separari a te.*
From the malignant enemy defend me.	*Ab hoste maligno defende me.*

In the hour of my death, call me

In hora mortis meae voca me

And bid me come to You,

Et iube me venire ad te,

That with Your saints I may praise You

Ut cum sanctis tuis laudem te

Forever and ever. Amen.

In saecula saeculorum. Amen.

Invitation

The *Anima Christi* or *Soul of Christ* prayer has long been popular with Catholics. It dates back to the early fourteenth century, 150 years before Saint Ignatius of Loyola recommended it in his *Spiritual Exercises,* thus ensuring that this beautiful prayer would not be lost over time.

What is the ageless appeal of the *Soul of Christ* prayer? Its warmth and familiarity with Jesus ease me into praying, especially if I feel dry or distracted. Right away, it leads me into my relationship with Christ. But the *Soul of Christ* is not just intensely personal. This timeless prayer also connects us with the great mysteries of our faith in a personal way that both comforts and challenges us. When I pray, "Body of Christ, save me," I make an act of faith in the Incarnation, the presence of Jesus in the Eucharist, and the mystery of our redemption. This rich prayer is well worth exploring deeply, not just for its history and recommendations from the saints (Saint Ignatius of Loyola, Blessed Peter Favre, Blessed James Alberione, among others), but also for its solid premises about the spiritual life that can nurture our spiritual growth.

Praying the *Soul of Christ* daily for many years has shaped my prayer life profoundly, helping me to:

- ⚜ nurture and foster my personal relationship with Christ—a relationship that is close, personal, and spiritually intimate, and that transforms me and my relationships with others;

- ⚜ pray with my whole self to Christ in both His humanity and divinity;

- ⚜ pray with the great mysteries of our faith—the Incarnation, the paschal mystery, the Eucharist, and Christ's saving love for us—in a way that connects with how I live my life here and now;

- ⚜ unite the desire of my heart to the desire of Jesus that I may be so transformed that I can say with Saint Paul: "For to me, living is Christ" (Phil 1:21).

The underlying premise that I find the most appealing in this prayer is its relational familiarity with Jesus. Sometimes we followers of Christ can make our faith overly formal, intellectual, or result-oriented. I know that I've fallen into the trap of focusing too much on adherence to doctrine or a strict moral system. Perhaps because doctrinal orthodoxy and observance of the commandments are somewhat measurable, we find reassurance when we can point to them as *proof* that we are faithful followers of Christ.

Knowing the Creed well and living the commandments are both important aspects of our response to Christ. They are part of the truth that He brings, freeing us from the intellectual errors and moral obstacles that can hinder or prevent a living encounter with Him. But the first priority of a follower of Christ is encountering

Him—an ongoing encounter with the Son of God that transforms our entire lives.

"Cafeteria Catholicism," where people choose to believe and live only those teachings or moral precepts that they find appealing, is a troubling symptom of a faith that hasn't been fully integrated with life. In a true encounter with Christ we recognize that our whole lives are to be centered in Him, like Saint Paul discovered on the way to Damascus. When we truly meet Christ, "cafeteria Catholicism" begins to lose its appeal because the will of God takes precedence— the will of God manifested in the Word of God and the Church's teaching. We find the strength to live God's will in our ongoing relationship with Jesus.

The heart of Christianity is encountering Jesus Christ, and Christian discipleship is about continually growing in union with Him. The focus of the *Soul of Christ* prayer is to live more deeply united with Jesus by our personal participation in the paschal mystery—Christ's suffering, death, and resurrection. The urgency of the petitions in this prayer reminds us that we *need* Christ and the salvation He brings us, and that our relationship is not one-dimensional.

Even when I'm suffering through a dry spell in my prayer, the *Soul of Christ* provides a personal connection and an "easy in" to my daily encounter with Jesus. The petitions help me to remember and acknowledge that the Jesus who suffered and died for me is present, listening to me, wanting to draw me closer to Himself. The confidence expressed in every line reminds me that Jesus wants to bless me with the fruits of His suffering, death, and resurrection so that He touches me, heals me, and saves me *today*. My prayers of petition become a thanksgiving to the risen Master who loves me so much.

Seven-year-old Danny was well prepared to receive his First Holy Communion. About a week before the big day, he asked his godmother if the TV reporters would interview him for the nightly news.

"Why?" asked his clueless godmother. "Why would the news reporters be there?"

"Because I'm going to receive Jesus for the first time!" the boy blurted out. "This is the most important day of my life until I get married!"

Sometimes a child's faith gives us clearer vision. Danny was right: the Eucharist *is* big news. Receiving the Eucharist is the most important event of our day or of our week, because the Eucharist shapes our entire life. The tremendous gift that Jesus gives us in the Eucharist—Himself—can completely transform us if we allow Christ to live and work freely in us.

The *Soul of Christ* is an ideal Eucharistic prayer, fostering that transformation in us. Traditionally, the *Soul of Christ* was recommended for praying after Communion, when it is sometimes easier to focus on our relationship with Christ.

Transformation in Christ is the key to the *Soul of Christ* prayer, and also to the spirituality of Saint Paul, who expresses this directly: "It is no longer I who live, but it is Christ who lives in me" (Gal 2:20). Saint Paul's letters are full of references to living in Christ, but many people today find his letters inaccessible. In the early twentieth century, the young Italian priest, James Alberione,[1] felt that Saint Paul's spirituality was what the Church needed—in his time and in the future millennium. Father Alberione was not only personally inspired by this great saint. He gave Saint Paul as protector, patron, and guide to the ten institutes of the Pauline Family he founded, entrusting them with the task of being "Saint Paul alive today." Thousands of members of the Pauline Family today strive to live Saint Paul's spirit as illumined and lived by Blessed James Alberione.

Blessed James develops the Pauline theme of life in Christ through the focal point of the description Jesus gave of Himself at the Last Supper: "I am the Way; I am Truth and Life" (Jn 14:6). By encouraging the Pauline Family to live Jesus as Way, Truth, and Life, Blessed James gives us a concrete and holistic way of understanding holiness and "life in Christ" in our daily lives:

- ⚓ Jesus is our Truth, who sanctifies our minds and gives us the gift of faith so that we can put on the mind of Christ.

- ⚓ Jesus is our Way, our Model, who invites us to walk with Him and imitate His example in doing the will of the Father. Jesus Way gives us the strength to love others—especially those who are "least"—in every situation.

- ⚓ Jesus is our Life, offering His life to save ours, seeking to draw us always deeper into the embrace of God so that we can love with the Heart of Christ.

Blessed James Alberione's holistic Pauline spirituality, which he drew from the Letters of Saint Paul, has inspired me as a Daughter of St. Paul and as I've prayed the *Soul of Christ* daily at his encouragement. Alberione's thoughts and insights are reflected here in these pages. I've also included some of Blessed James Alberione's most beautiful, privately written Eucharistic prayers, making some of them available in English for the first time.

My hope for those who read this book is that the *Soul of Christ* will become for you, too, a treasure that will enrich your spiritual journey, nurture a fuller transformation in Christ, and engender a greater joy in the marvelous gift of the Holy Eucharist.

Suggestions for using this book

Soul of Christ: Meditations on a Timeless Prayer can be used for spiritual reading, for meditation or personal prayer, and for Eucharistic adoration. Each chapter considers one petition of the prayer. To make it easy to use, each chapter is divided into two main sections.

The first section is a reflection on each phrase of the particular petition from a Eucharistic perspective. The wording of this prayer is so rich that the reflection is meant to be simply a starting place for your own contemplation of Christ and the mysteries of our faith.

The second section explores the petition more prayerfully in the light of a particular Scripture passage. You can continue reading this section straight through—as you have the previous one—or you can use it for praying an hour of adoration with the assistance of the additional notes in the margins.

The three-movement hour of adoration was developed by Blessed James Alberione. In the first movement of the Pauline Hour of Adoration—*Adoring Jesus Truth*—you are invited to pray with the word of God. The Scripture passage is chosen to enrich your reflections on the theme of the petition from the *Soul of Christ* prayer. During this time of profound listening, allow the word of God to shape your thoughts and attitudes.

The second movement, *Following Jesus Way*, gives you the opportunity to reflect on your spiritual journey in the light of the Scripture passage: the ways that God is at work in your life, your thanksgiving to God for His loving Providence, the challenges that you face, and the invitations that God holds out to you to change and grow closer to Him. Through the questions offered for an examination of conscience, you can ponder God's loving invitations and how you have responded to them, ask God's forgiveness for your sinfulness, and pray for the grace and strength to respond more fully to God's love in the future.

The third movement in the Pauline hour, *In Union with Jesus*, is a time for prayer of union with Christ our Life. Thematically selected prayers are offered that can help you to deepen your union with Jesus; offer Him your hopes, joys, sufferings, and efforts; and learn how to more fully share God's love with others in your daily life. This is a time for *prayer of the heart*, when you and Jesus can speak heart-to-heart about your desires and the needs of the world, offering all with Jesus to the Father.

The Appendix, *How to Make a Pauline Hour of Adoration*, contains further explanation of the Pauline Hour of Adoration.

The hours of adoration can be used individually or in a group. When prayed individually, the prepared "hours" are meant to be adapted to your needs—the material is more of an outline or resource to help you begin or deepen your adoration. For group use, the leader can simply add hymns and times of silence to allow each adorer to deepen the readings and reflections. A little additional preparation can enrich the group prayer, such as inviting adorers to bring their own Bibles or requesting someone besides the group leader to read the Scripture reading aloud. Further suggestions for group use are provided in the Appendix. To make preparation for group adoration easier, a free downloadable group handout for each hour of adoration is available at: www.pauline. org/mariepaulcurley.

The foundation of the *Soul of Christ* prayer is woven as a recurring theme throughout the pages of each meditation: God's saving love for us revealed in Christ Jesus. Christ's love for us is absolutely faithful, limitless, and unconditional—we are cherished for who we are, and at the same time we are invited to grow more fully in union with Him.

May our meditations together on this powerful prayer guide each of us toward the embrace of Christ's unfathomable love, so that we not only celebrate and adore Jesus in the Eucharist, but we live *Eucharistic lives.* If we each become *little eucharists,* Christ can work through us to transform the world with His amazing love.

⟡ CHAPTER 1 ⟡

Soul of Christ, sanctify me

The beautiful *Anima Christi* prayer begins with a deeply personal petition that immediately draws us into a genuine encounter with Christ. In fact, each of the first six petitions of this prayer focus our attention on a specific aspect of Christ's humanity, similar to our recalling the cherished qualities of a friend or loved one. This first line delves into the deep desire of Christ's soul to encounter us and be united with us.

"Soul of Christ"

"Soul of Christ" is a unique, familiar way to address Jesus, and it sets a personal tone for the entire prayer. This might not be obvious at first glance, because "soul" is a term with many nuances. From a Catholic perspective, the soul is understood as the spiritual part of the person that not only gives life to the body but makes one the unique person he or she is; the soul is the innermost part of the person. In the context of the many petitions that focus on different aspects of Christ—His body, blood, wounds, and sufferings

9

—"soul" refers not to a disembodied view of Christ but rather to His innermost humanity united to His divinity—the *essence* of who Jesus is.

What a direct, familiar, and powerful way to begin our prayer! In doing so, we express our faith in two incredible mysteries:

- ⚜ The Real Presence of Jesus in the Eucharist, Body, Blood, soul, and divinity. (During the Mass, Jesus becomes truly, really present in the Eucharist under the appearance of bread and wine.)

- ⚜ Jesus wants so much to be close to us that He makes Himself incredibly accessible in the Holy Eucharist. Jesus is physically present at *every* celebration of the Eucharist and remains in the tabernacles of thousands of Catholic churches throughout the world.

If we read the Gospels closely, we discover many instances where Christ expresses His yearning to be close to us (e.g., Mt 4:19, 11:28; Lk 19:5; Jn 12:32, 15). When we pray the "Soul of Christ," we respond to this deep longing of the soul of Jesus.

What does it mean to encounter someone's soul?

Though my father passed away over ten years ago, I still miss the way he used to look at me. When I would arrive home for a visit or right before I would leave, my dad usually did not say anything, but his eyes would fill with deep emotion, and he would just gaze at me. I would feel so loved, so at home, so connected with him. I think that in those timeless moments I glimpsed my dad's soul, his very essence: the fruitful love for his family that had come to define him, his deep-down goodness, and the way that his love shaped me into who I am.

Jesus looks at each of us with such a gaze of love, but it is an infinitely greater love.

Sometimes the Eucharistic presence of Jesus is silent. He offers us a humble, unspoken love that without complaint undergoes the limitations of the form of bread for the sake of being near us. His quiet presence listens attentively to our distress or distraction, even when we barely acknowledge Him. Yet, when we are able to pay attention, the quiet presence of Jesus can deluge us with the sense of being loved, embraced, and gazed upon with delight.

Praying with the word of God before Jesus in the Eucharist is one of the most vital ways to pray. In His word, Jesus offers us concrete guidance in our day-to-day living, always adapted to just what we need when we are able to listen deeply. The word transforms us, little by little, making us more Christ-like.

" . . . sanctify me"

"Sanctify" means to make holy. All of us are called to holiness, but a true understanding of holiness is elusive, even mysterious.

Reflect a few moments on what holiness is to you personally. How are you called to be holy?

One way to make the idea of holiness concrete is to think of three people we know whom we would describe as holy. Why would we describe them that way? What do they have in common?

Our spiritual tradition describes holiness in many ways:

⚜ union with God

- ⚓ abundance or fullness of life
- ⚓ freedom
- ⚓ the perfection of charity
- ⚓ to be "of God"
- ⚓ being Christ-like

As the Son of God, Jesus *is* Divine Love who created us, recreates us, and saves us. In the Incarnation, the Second Person of the Blessed Trinity entered human history and took on our human nature, including a human soul, to draw us closer to Himself, to sanctify us.

We can best understand what holiness means by contemplating Jesus during His life on earth. With His human soul, will, mind, and heart, the Son of God shares in the entirety of our human experience and shows us how we too can live in loving union with the Father. The entire life of Jesus—from His humble birth and hidden life at Nazareth to His suffering, death, and resurrection—is our Way to holiness.

Jesus *is* the Love of God made human, visible, and tangible. The work of the Church is to be the presence of Jesus extended throughout history so that, especially in the sacraments, we have a way to grow closer to Him. Every sacrament is a miraculous encounter with God's love. But Jesus encounters us in an especially marvelous way in the Eucharist, where He waits for us.

At the Last Supper, Jesus invites his disciples to *abide* in Him: to love and be loved as Jesus loves and is loved by the Father. These invitations to holiness are memorialized at the Last Supper and in every Eucharist we celebrate. Contemplating this personal invitation to union with Jesus during times of adoration can transform our attitude and participation at every Mass.

Our unique call to holiness

We all share a common call, a common vocation, to holiness. But each of us is to live that call uniquely, to shine in an unrepeatable way with the radiance of the face of God. In his book, *Wishful Thinking: A Seeker's ABC*, Christian writer Frederick Buechner writes, "The place God calls you to is the place where your deep gladness and the world's deep hunger meet."[1] God has given us to the world just as much as He has given the world to us. In this light, it is helpful to pray with Blessed John Henry Newman's beautiful meditation about the mission that is particular and unique to each of us:

> God has created me to do Him some definite service;
> He has committed some work to me which He has not
>   committed to another.
> I have my mission—I never may know it in this life, but I shall
>   be told it in the next.
> Somehow I am necessary for His purposes.[2]

Someone—perhaps "many someones"—in this world needs us to be who we are called to be, to love as we are called to love. The world desperately needs us to be saints.

God gives us the precious gift of one lifetime. What a tragedy it would be to waste our potential, to *never* know the joy of expressing and sharing our unique "voice" and gifts with the world. Yet it is deceptively easy to waste our life on things that are good but are not part of our deep call to holiness.

We live our deepest call when we are fully ourselves, when we strive to be and embrace *who* God calls us to be and *how* God calls us to be. It's hard work to say "yes" to our deeper call over and over, to turn away from sin, to ignore distractions, and to tune the melody of our life so that our authentic voice—in all its God-given purity, clarity, and power—rings out through the world.

One woman who lived an unusual way to holiness is Blessed Margaret of Castello. Born in the thirteenth century with numerous physical disabilities (blindness, lameness, short stature, and hunchbacked), she was imprisoned for years by her family because they were ashamed of her. Finally, they brought her to a shrine in the hopes that she would be healed. When she wasn't, they abandoned her there. But others took Margaret in and came to admire her. Eventually, Margaret became a Dominican tertiary known not for her unusual appearance, but for her prayer and charity to others.

Margaret could have spent her entire life in self-pity, resentment, or chasing after cures. Instead, she sought to serve others, rejoicing in the gift of her life, her call to holiness, and the unique opportunities she was given to serve others and to offer her sufferings to Jesus. Her unique vocation to love triumphed over the adversities she faced.

As the saints show us, being holy means we become most fully ourselves. Yet holiness itself is not something we can earn, achieve, or win. Instead, holiness is God's gift; it comes about in our relationship with God. Our part in becoming holy is to respond to grace, to let God work freely in us. That's why Jesus invites us as His disciples to leave aside our fear and, instead of trying to achieve holiness on our own, to share in His holiness. He invites us to immerse all of our being in God.

Soul of Christ, sanctify me. In this petition we pray for union with Christ, that through us our despairing, desolate world may receive the hope and love of Christ Jesus.

The second part of each chapter connects the petition with a passage from Scripture. You may use this second part (hereinafter indicated by a footnote) to make an hour of adoration by praying with the suggested material set apart in the boxes, or you can simply continue reading and skip over the additional suggestions.

In the Light of God's Word

Theme for Holy Hour:
Jesus, Our Way to Holiness

Suggested opening hymn: "Soul of My Savior" (traditional).
Quiet time for personal adoration.

Adoring Jesus in His Word

"Do not let your hearts be troubled. Believe in God, believe also in me. In my Father's house there are many dwelling places. If it were not so, would I have told you that I go to prepare a place for you? And if I go and prepare a place for you, I will come again and will take you to myself, so that where I am, there you may be also. And you know the way to the place where I am going." Thomas said to him, "Lord, we do not know where you are going. How can we know the way?" Jesus said to him, "I am the way, and the truth, and the life. No one comes to the Father except through me. If you know me, you will know my Father also. From now on you do know him and have seen him" (Jn 14:1–7).

At the Last Supper, Jesus has come almost to the end of His earthly journey with His disciples. He knows their hearts and sees their questions and the struggles they will face after His crucifixion. So He

Pause for five to ten minutes of quiet reflection.
As our Way, our Eucharistic Master accompanies us on the journey of our lives.

offers them the most accessible way to holiness: union with Himself. When Jesus says here, "I am the way, and the truth, and the life," is He not referring to Himself especially in the Holy Eucharist? Jesus offers us Himself as a *way in* to the privileged, inner life of the Trinity!

He walks before us

In both celebration and adoration, we contemplate the life of Jesus and we . . .

- ⚜ stare into the stable at Bethlehem, marveling at the selfless love of the Second Person of the Blessed Trinity revealed in an Infant's smile;

- ⚜ peer into the humble poverty of a simple home in Nazareth, where the Son of God sleeps on the ground;

- ⚜ marvel at the obedience of a beloved Son who dedicates Himself to the ordinary drudgery of work and to loving attentiveness to His family;

- ⚜ wonder at His single-hearted, inimitable union with His Father;

- ⚜ rejoice in a young rabbi's unwavering dedication to the mission of announcing the kingdom of God;

- ⚜ are intrigued by His withdrawing from the intense pressures of His mission to seek the company of His Father in prayer;

- ⚜ feel comfort at the outpouring of healing and mercy on all whom Jesus encounters;

- ⚜ stand wordless at His total surrender to His Father in the outpouring of His very life for us on the cross;

⚓ bask in the radiant joy of the resurrection.

As we pray with these mysteries in the life of Christ, we know that, if we seek to live in Christ, we too will sometimes find ourselves at the foot of the cross. But moments of pain and desolation can become privileged opportunities for union with Christ. We will never be alone. Jesus walks with us now and at every moment of our lives.

> After you finish reading the reflection, allow a few minutes of silence, then pray an act of faith, such as the Apostles' or Nicene Creed.

He walks with us

Following Jesus Way

In the Mass, Jesus offers us the light of His word when we read Scripture and the nourishment of His own Body and Blood every time we receive Communion.

Yet, if Jesus offers us so many graces and wants our holiness so much, why aren't we already holy? Because holiness happens in relationship. On one side is God who reaches out to us—our God who loves us into being and consistently offers us grace. On the other side, we stand as sinful human beings, free to welcome, reject, deny, or resist God's embrace. Holiness isn't easy; it's choosing to love above all else. A part of us resists because we know that love always includes suffering—at the very least, the pain mixed with the joy of self-giving. For most of us, holiness is a journey of baby steps, as we gradually let go of our resistances and slowly open ourselves more fully to God's transforming love.

Blessed James Alberione wrote, "The action of sanctifying the soul consists in our transformation into God through the food which is Jesus Christ. We are to nourish ourselves daily on Jesus Christ, Way, Truth, and Life."[3]

What holds me back from giving myself completely to the God who gives Himself to me? How does Jesus invite me to grow in holiness? How can I respond to His love for me?

> Pause here to reflect on these questions, silently making a personal examination of conscience or personal examen.[4]
> Before continuing, pray an act of contrition (such as the Lamb of God).

Although we recognize our sinfulness and unworthiness, we don't let them stop us from offering ourselves to Jesus. Jesus doesn't wait for us to become good before He comes to us. Instead, He is already there for us in word and Eucharist, wanting to be with us at every moment of our journey.

Light, humility, silence, acceptance, a faithful ear, nourishment, unconditional love—these are all expressions of His faithful presence, a presence that will never abandon us and always calls us to greater love and holiness.

> For the ways Jesus has been and will be present in your life, thank Him in your own words or with a favorite prayer, such as the Glory be or the Te Deum.

He is the One we walk toward

When we love others, we want the best for them. We start to want what they want. Jesus loves us so

> **In Union with Jesus**
> In your own words, express to Jesus your desire to be united to Him.

much that He wants our greatest good, our holiness. Jesus knows that we will be happiest if we share fully in His own life.

Praying the words "Soul of Christ, sanctify me" reminds us to begin to surrender to this desire of Jesus. This beautiful prayer hones our desires so that our hearts start to beat in sync with the heart of Jesus. We start to want what He wants for us: holiness. As we pray for the desire of Jesus to come to pass *in us,* we begin to let go of our resistance. (Or at least, we pray for the grace to let go of resistance.)

Jesus our Way invites us to share so deeply in His life that we begin to share in His own relationship with the Father and we begin to *be* His presence in the world. Let us make this desire of union with Jesus our own, not just in this moment of prayerful reflection, but throughout our day and week. At the end of our lives, we will be able to look forward to the bliss of a never-ending, perfect union with God in Christ.

The following prayer is a series of petitions for sanctifying every aspect of our lives. We may wish to carry the sentiments of this profound prayer for transformation in Christ with us as we return to daily life.

Appeals to Jesus Master by Blessed James Alberione

> Pray this prayer slowly, contemplating Jesus as your Truth, Way, and Life while asking for the grace to live in Him.

Jesus Master, sanctify my mind and increase my faith.

Jesus, teaching in the Church, draw everyone to Yourself.

Jesus Master, deliver me from error, empty thoughts and eternal blindness.

Jesus Way between the Father and us, I offer everything to You and await everything from You.

Jesus Way of sanctity, help me imitate You faithfully.

Jesus Way, may I respond wholeheartedly to the Father's call
to holiness.

Jesus Life, live in me so that I may live in You.

Jesus Life, do not ever permit anything to separate me
from You.

Jesus Life, grant that I may live eternally in the joy of
Your love.

Jesus Truth, may You shine in
the world through me.

Jesus Way, may I be a faithful
mirror of Your example
for others.

Jesus Life, may I be a channel
of Your grace and consolation
to others.[5]

Conclude your hour of
adoration with a hymn, such
as "Song of St. Patrick,"
(based on "St. Patrick's
Breastplate") composed by
Marty Haugen.

✥ Chapter 2 ✥

Body of Christ, save me

The second petition of the *Anima Christi* prayer uses a phrase with multiple meanings: "Body of Christ." This chapter focuses on how Jesus saves us by sharing our humanity.

"Body of Christ"

The phrase "Body of Christ" acknowledges the mystery of the Incarnation: out of love for us, the Son of God took on our human nature. The Second Person of the Blessed Trinity took on the limitations of our humanity to draw close to us and to save us. By itself, this one petition can be repeated as an act of heartfelt praise and thanksgiving.

With a human body, Jesus enters fully into our human experience. Although completely free from sin, He did not exempt Himself from the limitations and sufferings of our human condition, including those caused by sin. During His life on earth, Jesus underwent fatigue, hunger, thirst, hard work, the heat of the day, and the chill of the night.

He experienced:

- ✤ being raised in a family within a small community of an oppressed people;
- ✤ the joy of being a beloved son;
- ✤ apprehension and excitement as He began His unique mission;
- ✤ the sorrow of frequent misunderstandings and rejections;
- ✤ anger against injustice and oppression;
- ✤ the terrors and sufferings of a horrific death;
- ✤ the spiritual desolation of feeling abandoned by His Father;
- ✤ the full surrender of His life into the hands of the Father.

Jesus, Son of God and Son of Man, calls Himself our Way and shows us how to be truly human, how to live as God's beloved. Sometimes we might experience our humanness as a source of weakness, something to despise or wish away. Who of us would choose hunger or fatigue? Jesus did.

For love of us, Jesus became truly human, fully sharing in the human condition, including limits of time and space. The next time we are frustrated by our limitations—perhaps when we run out of time or energy—we can remember that the Son of God lived within those same limits. After only three years dedicated to His public mission, His earthly life was cut short when He was thirty-three.

Every human experience—no matter how trivial, difficult, tragic, passionate, or senseless—can lead us to holiness when we seek to live it in union with Christ:

⚜ When we are angry, we can remember Jesus chasing the moneymakers out of the sacred space of the Temple.

⚜ When we seek relief from the burden of work, we remember Jesus laboring as an ordinary woodworker with His foster father Joseph.

⚜ When we grieve a great loss in our life, the tears of Jesus over the death of his friend Lazarus mingle with ours.

⚜ When we suffer from want—physical or emotional—we remember Jesus having nowhere to lay His head, surrounded by goodhearted but clueless disciples.

⚜ When we suffer misunderstanding or betrayal, we ask Jesus, betrayed with a kiss by one of His closest followers, to stay with us and teach us strength and forgiveness.

⚜ When we feel overwhelmed, we can imitate Jesus, who sought out His Father in prayer in the depths of the night.

" . . . save me"

When we feel the misery of our human condition, we desire salvation. Sometimes, however, especially when things are going well, we may not feel the need to be saved.

Salvation is not a dry theological concept, nor is "being saved" a one-time event. This petition reminds us that we constantly need to be saved, just as we constantly need to be converted. Our wounded human condition offers us countless temptations to turn in on ourselves and away from God and others. Original sin deeply injured our human nature with enthralling tendencies toward the seven capital sins: pride, avarice, envy, anger, lust, gluttony, and sloth. Certain circumstances—like suffering, loss, transition, or addiction—

intensify our tendency toward sin, despite our pretense that we only rarely *need* God.

The truth is that we need God every day. We rely on His Providence for everything, even our next breath. If we just try to get by and stay comfortable, if we settle for mediocrity and avoid the challenges of life and the sufferings of others, we may not feel the need for God. If instead we seek to live our call to holiness, then we quickly realize how weak we are and how much we depend on Jesus, who constantly offers God's saving love.

"To be saved" is to live in constant awareness of God's love for us, and to faithfully choose to live as God's beloved, even at great cost. "To be saved" is a daily—often moment-by-moment—choice to allow Jesus to love us and to love through us.

In the powerful 1996 film, *Marvin's Room,*[1] Bessie (portrayed by Diane Keaton) and Lee (portrayed by Meryl Streep) are two sisters who respond in opposite ways when their father suffers an incapacitating stroke. Lee flees home, while Bessie makes the difficult but loving choice to give up her own dreams and return home to take care of their father, who cannot sit up, walk, speak, or understand most of what's going on around him. For seventeen years Bessie cares for her father full-time—years of loneliness, fatigue, and struggle. When Lee finally comes to visit, Bessie tries to explain how blessed she has been. Lee misunderstands and agrees that their dad loves Bessie very much—which does not make sense, since their father has not been able to express anything for almost twenty years. Bessie clarifies that she is blessed because she has *been able to love someone else* so much.

This is grace at work in the life of an ordinary woman who has discovered both her personal mission and her deepest fulfillment in self-sacrificing love. This is a woman who has allowed grace to *save* her, even in the long and lonely struggle of caring for her father.

Like Bessie, we are invited to see the challenges in our lives as opportunities to be saved, as openings for grace to take root more deeply in us. *Body of Christ, save me!* becomes not just a prayer of praise, but also of heartfelt longing.*

In the Light of God's Word

Theme for Holy Hour:
The Word Made Flesh

Suggested opening hymn: "At the Name of Jesus," written by Caroline Maria Noel (based on Phil 2:5–7) or "Jesus the Lord," by Roc O'Connor, SJ (based on Phil 2:5–11; Acts 17:28).

Quiet time for personal adoration.

Adoring Jesus in His Word

"They came to Bethsaida. Some people brought a blind man to him and begged him to touch him. He took the blind man by the hand and led him out of the village; and when he had put saliva on his eyes and laid his hands on him, he asked him, "Can you see anything?" And the man looked up and said, "I can see people, but they look like trees, walking." Then Jesus laid his hands on his eyes again; and he looked

---

* You may use this second part of the chapter to make an hour of adoration by praying with the additional suggestions set apart in the boxes, or you can simply continue reading.

intently and his sight was restored, and he saw everything clearly. Then he sent him away to his home, saying, "Do not even go into the village." (Mk 8:22–26)

The Gospel of Mark recounts many unique details in this unusual miracle. As we reflect on the human gestures Jesus uses to heal the man who is blind—gestures that He fills with grace—we ponder how Jesus graces the ordinary human moments of our lives.

Jesus Heals Through Human Touch

People bring the blind man to Jesus and beg Him to touch and heal him. Jesus does so, unexpectedly. First, Jesus takes him by the hand and leads him apart from the others. What a comforting gesture—to offer guidance and personal connection to someone immersed in the dark. Did Jesus want to offer him the dignity of privacy, or the opportunity to speak in confidence? Perhaps Jesus wanted to allay the man's fears and help him to grow in faith so that he could be healed more fully. While we can only guess at the motivation of Jesus, this beautiful, personal moment has parallels in our lives. When we are lost and blinded by our fears, prejudices, or assumptions, Jesus takes us by the hand and leads us to where He can heal us. How close Jesus comes to us in our weakness!

Then Jesus uses His saliva and the touch of His hands to heal—surprising physical gestures that Jesus repeats until the man receives full sight. Jesus can work through anything in our lives, even ordinary physical details. We cannot predict *what* God will use to reveal Himself to us and to save us, and we cannot discount what we perceive to be human and messy: saliva, human touch, or the ups and downs of our relationships with others.

This miracle reveals a dramatic Gospel truth: Jesus does not just come to us in the "big" moments of our lives but in the daily stuff of life, *in* the gifts of God's creation—other

> After a few moments of personal reflection, pray John 1:1–18 as an act of faith and adoration.

people, bread, wine, oil, water. Most radiantly, Jesus comes to us in the Church, where together as the Body of Christ we celebrate the Eucharist. In the Eucharist, Jesus uses common bread and wine and transforms them into His own Body and Blood in order to give us Himself and unite us with each other.

Jesus's Desire to Save

> **Following Jesus Way**

Unless we have suffered from blindness ourselves, we may not fully appreciate the gift of sight. Being healed of blindness restores the possibility of living a full and fruitful

> Take a few moments to thank Jesus for the ways He has already worked His saving power in your life.

life—a powerful metaphor for being saved.

Praying this petition—*Body of Christ, save me*—encourages us to reflect on the tremendous saving love of God for us. While we may not always feel the urgency in this petition, let us ask the Lord's help to recognize how we need healing.

- All of us suffer from blind spots and weaknesses. What blindness or weakness do I bring to Jesus today to be healed? How do I need to be saved today?

> Choose one question and spend time with it, allowing it to lead you into a deep examination of conscience.

- ⚜ Do I want physical or spiritual healing? Perhaps I sense hardness in my heart, or an interior resistance that needs transformation.

- ⚜ Do I long for something more in my life—to move from "being stuck" in the dry rut of routine to the freedom to respond to God's new invitations?

- ⚜ Is there an injustice in my family, neighborhood, or society that needs the power of God's grace to address or confront?

- ⚜ To whom do I want to extend God's saving love today? Perhaps I want to use my hands to imitate the compassionate touch of Jesus, or my tongue to speak lovingly, as Jesus would do.

We can take a few moments to bring to the Lord something in us that needs to be saved and healed, allowing ourselves to be touched by His love.

> The greatest healing we can receive is from our sinfulness. We pray for this grace.

We are called to be God's healing presence in the world. In our humanness, this union of body and soul, we can touch each other in ways that would not be possible if we were just spiritual beings. We can come to appreciate—as God already does—the gift of our hands, reaching out in kindness; the gift of our tongues, warmly speaking the precise words another person needs to hear; the gift of our presence, alleviating loneliness and building a sense of family and communion; the gift of our physical strength, rubbing shoulders in a common effort. Every aspect of our physical being—including our ability to give ourselves in love fully to a spouse—is a tremendous gift that we both experience ourselves and offer to another. As Saint Paul says, "Do you not know that your body is a temple of the Holy Spirit within you, which you have from God, and that you are not your own? For you were bought with a price; therefore glorify God in your body" (I Cor 6:19–20). We pray for this grace: to glorify God with our whole being, bodies and souls.

We ask for the grace of healing and light through a prayer to the Holy Spirit, perhaps with the familiar hymn, "Come, Holy Ghost," words attributed to Rabanus Maurus, translated by Edward Caswall.

In Union with Christ

In Union with Jesus

Christ has no body now upon
the earth but yours,
no hands but yours,
no feet but yours.
Yours are the eyes through which Christ's compassion looks
upon the world.
Yours are the lips with which His love has to speak.
Yours are the hands with which He is to bless us now,
and yours the feet with which He is to go about doing good
through His Church, which is His Body.

— often attributed to Saint Teresa of Avila, but origins unknown

During His earthly life, Jesus used His hands for all the usual daily activities of His time—to labor, hug, heal, share, eat, bless, and break bread for others. We pray that whatever actions or gestures we make

In your mind, picture the actions of the rest of your day, and ask Jesus to work through your hands, your lips, your body, in each circumstance.

with our hands and our bodies—no matter how ordinary—can be sanctified by Jesus's holy hands.

Blessed James Alberione spoke of holiness as allowing God to take flesh in us: "To become saints, we have to incarnate God in ourselves."[2] For Alberione, the font of holiness is the Eucharist: "It is in Communion that our natural life is replaced by the divine life of Jesus Christ. Grafted into Jesus, we will . . . speak and think as Jesus; live of Jesus; die with Jesus. We will have no other ideal than to be a living image of Jesus Christ: 'I live now not with my own life but with the life of Christ who lives in me' (Gal 2:20). Then the Mass will leave a profound impression on us."[3]

> Resolve to ask for the grace to *live of Jesus* the next time you participate at Mass and receive Communion.

In adoration and at Mass, we can pray these words, *Body of Christ, save me*, asking that our bodies and our entire beings are freed from the power of sin and transformed into the likeness of Christ. The following prayer from the personal journal of Blessed James Alberione can help us to unpack this petition even further.

> If you have time, pray this prayer line by line, pausing to reflect and pray for the grace to sanctify your heart, your ears, your mouth, and so forth. Feel free to add your own petitions as well.

May I love with Your heart, Jesus,
May I hear only with Your ears.
May I savor what You delight in.
May my hands become Your hands.
May my feet follow in Your footsteps.

May I pray with Your prayer.
May I treat others the way You
    treat them.
May I celebrate Mass the way
    You immolated Yourself.
May I be in You and You in me
    to the point that I disappear.
Deign to make use of this
    tongue to sing to God for all ages,
of this heart to love Him,
of this most unfortunate sinner to proclaim You;
"I am the Good Shepherd; I desire mercy." [4]

Conclude your hour with a spiritual communion and a hymn such as "Be Thou My Vision," from ancient Gaelic and translated by Eleanor Hull, or "Bread, Blessed and Broken" by Michael B. Lynch.

⚜ CHAPTER 3 ⚜

Body of Christ, save me
(continued)

In this chapter, we continue to pray with the petition, *Body of Christ, save me*, focusing particularly on the saving presence of Jesus in the Eucharist—Jesus celebrated, adored, and lived—and how His saving presence transforms us as Church into the living Body of Christ in time and space.

"Body of Christ"

Two of the greatest mysteries that define our faith are referred to in this simple phrase. Both are about God coming closer to us: the Incarnation (the Son of God taking on our humanity to save us) and the Eucharist (the Son of God taking on the form of bread and wine to become our food and drink, to draw us into the embrace of the Trinity). One profound connection between these two mysteries is how much God loves us.

The life, passion, death, and resurrection of Jesus are the ways that He—as Son of God and Son of Man—could physically express both His saving love for us and the loving will of the Most Holy Trinity that we be saved. The Eucharist is where we can touch and taste the love of God.

Because of routine, disillusionment, passivity, ignorance, or distraction we can come to take the mystery of the Eucharist for granted. We can forget what a great gift the Eucharist is. When we do, Mass can even seem a rote, tiresome duty. But to take part in the Eucharistic Mystery of Love is really an incredible privilege, no matter how we are feeling in the moment.

At bare minimum, participating at Mass is a way to praise and thank God for sending His Son to save us and to receive His saving love. But we are not called to live as "minimum Catholics." Instead, we are invited to *intensify* our participation in the Eucharistic Mystery—at Mass and during Eucharistic adoration:

- ✣ by adoring Jesus really present in the Eucharist—Body, Blood, soul, and divinity;
- ✣ by uniting ourselves to Jesus in His self-offering;
- ✣ by allowing Jesus to transform and send us as messengers of His love to others.

Jesus perpetuates the sacrifice of the cross through the Eucharistic sacrifice. How can we remain indifferent before the *Real Presence* of the Son of God who loves us to the point of brokenness and death? Just as during His earthly life Jesus risked hatred, persecution, and execution, in His vulnerable presence in the Eucharist, Jesus risks being ignored, disrespected, hated, and reviled. Wafers of bread that can be broken and cups of wine that can be spilled are the Eucharistic sign of our omnipotent God becoming vulnerable for us. A fragile wafer of bread *contains* the Alpha and the Omega, the Lord of all creation. This fragility is how Jesus chooses to save us. This selfless fragility is what makes Him so accessible to us. Let us adore His Eucharistic humility, hiddenness, vulnerability, silence, self-giving . . .

A few years ago when I was making retreat, it really came home to me how much I had let fear stifle me throughout my life. But I didn't have the humility to simply accept my fear and offer it to Jesus. Instead, I fell into the trap of shame and became deeply discouraged. If I was so full of fear, how could Christ love me and continue to call me to be a sister who communicates His love?

In this despondent frame of mind, I participated in midday Mass. I don't remember the readings—I'm not sure I even heard them. I do remember the rising desperation that tightened my chest throughout the Eucharistic Prayer. Then it was time for Communion. Since there were no Eucharistic ministers, Father indicated that he would like me to distribute Communion. Reluctantly and struggling internally, I went up to the altar. I received the Host in my hand and held Jesus. *What difference will it make?* was my first thought. *My sinfulness and fear will block Christ's grace.*

Jesus, Lamb of God, I adore You, I tried to pray. *But I am not worthy to receive You! How can You even tolerate coming to me in Communion?* As I lifted the Host closer, I could see how thin that Host was, how frail! A piece had broken off so that the Host was not perfectly round. It was even crumbly around the edges. *Like me,* I realized. Something shifted inside of me. If Jesus could transform such a humble thing as a broken wafer of bread into His Body, couldn't He transform me?

Those few seconds brushed eternity. I received Jesus very humbly, accepting His love for me, frail and fearful as I am. I begged Him to transform me and to work through my weakness. Jesus's frailty in the Eucharistic Host had helped me to receive His love for me—in and even through my weaknesses.

In every Communion, we are offered an opportunity that could make even the angels jealous: we are physically, tangibly united with Jesus; and if we are receptive, we are saved, sanctified, transformed. In adoration, we can take the quiet time we need to draw close to the One who has first come close to us. Each time we encounter Jesus in the Eucharist, His saving grace can enter us more fully and transform us, little by little.

" . . . save me, save us"

Jesus in the Eucharist does not just come to us individually. Saint Paul describes the Church as Christ's Mystical Body, with Christ as Head and the People of God as members. Perhaps we could sometimes pray, "Body of Christ, save *us*," aware that Jesus wants to continue His presence and saving mission through all the members of the Church He instituted.

In His priestly prayer, Jesus links His urgent plea to the Father for our salvation with His intense appeal that we be brought into communion with each other: "That they may all be one" (Jn 17:21). As members of the Body of Christ, we are not only united with Jesus but with each other in Him. Our adoption as children of God makes us brothers and sisters. Our differences, no matter how big, are surpassed by all we share in Christ.

As Church, formed by the Eucharistic Jesus into the Body of Christ, we are called to live the Eucharistic virtues that Jesus displayed so lovingly at the washing of the feet at the Last Supper: a silent presence that lovingly welcomes everyone, that forgives, that is available to everyone, that gives of self so that others may live.

Raymond was an ordinary, mischievous Polish boy, yet his mother witnessed his gradual maturation into a young man who wanted to give his life to Christ. As a teen, he entered the Franciscans and took the name Maximilian. He founded new friaries, developed the Franciscan mission, and was known to have a special love for Mary, the Immaculate. When the Nazis invaded Poland, Maximilian did his best to protect the friars and the Polish refugees—the majority of whom were Jews. Eventually, he was taken to the death camp of Auschwitz, where he was treated especially brutally because he did not hide the fact that he was a priest.

When ten men were unjustly condemned to death by starvation, one cried out in desperation that his wife and sons would never see him again. Maximilian stepped forward and offered to take his place. He died as a martyr of charity—offering his own life to save another's.

Saint Maximilian Kolbe's story stuns us; yet, in every Eucharist, we celebrate that Jesus has done even more for us! While we may not be called to lay down our lives for another as dramatically as Saint Maximilian did, we are called to spend ourselves in love—to truly love one another, even at great cost.*

---

* You may use this second part of the chapter to make an hour of adoration by praying with the additional suggestions set apart in the boxes, or you can simply continue reading.

In the Light of God's Word

Theme for Holy Hour:

Jesus, Center of Our Lives

Suggested opening hymn: "Center of My Life," refrain text and music composed by Paul Inwood, verses are Psalm 16. Spend some time in silent adoration.

Adoring Jesus in His Word

When the hour came, he took his place at the table, and the apostles with him. He said to them, "I have eagerly desired to eat this Passover with you before I suffer; for I tell you, I will not eat it until it is fulfilled in the kingdom of God." Then he took a cup, and after giving thanks he said, "Take this and divide it among yourselves; for I tell you that from now on I will not drink of the fruit of the vine until the kingdom of God comes." Then he took a loaf of bread, and when he had given thanks, he broke it and gave it to them, saying, "This is my body, which is given for you. Do this in remembrance of me." And he did the same with the cup after supper, saying, "This cup that is poured out for you is the new covenant in my blood. But see, the one who betrays me is with me, and his hand is on the table. For the Son of Man is going as it has been determined, but woe to that one by whom he is betrayed!" (Lk 22:14–22)

Pause for silent reflection.

In the Gospels, the institution of the Eucharist is such a momentous event that, as with the crucifixion, the Gospel writers tell it tersely without commentary. Yet every word and gesture of Jesus is significant, as He must have been acutely aware of what He was doing. Let us prayerfully consider the words of institution, repeated at every Eucharistic Celebration.

This is my body . . .

Jesus gives thanks, breaks the loaf, and changes it into His Body. Then, He literally offers His Body to the disciples as their food, His Blood as their drink. Jesus wants to be so close to us that He is our food and drink, that He becomes us and we become Him.

It stunned the saints to understand the intimacy that Jesus wants with us, His all-too-sinful followers. Yet, Jesus is clear that this closeness is what He wants: "I have eagerly desired to eat this Passover with you." Every Eucharistic Celebration contains this intense eagerness of Jesus to become one with us.

We are called to make our entire lives Eucharistic, to make the Eucharist the center of our lives. How can we do this, practically speaking?

Blessed James Alberione encouraged the practice of making the Mass the center of our day (or of our week, if we participate at Sunday Mass):

"Center the whole day in the Eucharist—this means to make the day Eucharistic. From noon to the next morning, prepare yourself by offering, sanctifying, and performing your various duties with hearts united to the Guest in the tabernacle. [After Mass] spend the morning in thanksgiving, radiating the fruits of holy joy, working 'through him, with him, in him' to the glory of the Blessed Trinity."[1]

Thus, the hours or days before we go to Mass become a time of preparation to receive Jesus, through prayers of love and desire and by offering our daily small sufferings to Him. And in the hours or days after Mass, we stir up in our hearts sentiments of joyful thanksgiving for all the gifts we have received, but most especially for the gift that Jesus makes of Himself.

This Act of Faith in the presence of Jesus in the Eucharist, written by Blessed James Alberione, is a beautiful prayer to prepare our hearts to receive Jesus.

> Take some additional time for your own personal reflection, then offer this Act of Faith and gratitude in the presence of Jesus in the Eucharist.

Act of Faith

Jesus, eternal Truth,
I believe You are really present in the bread and wine.
You are here with Your Body, Blood, soul and divinity.
I hear Your invitation: "I am the living bread descended from
    heaven"; "take and eat; this is My Body."
I believe, Lord and Master,
but strengthen my weak faith.[2]

. . . *given for you*

> Following Jesus Way

At the very moment at the Last Supper that Jesus gives Himself fully to His disciples, He also tells them that He is giving Himself fully *for* them—and for all of us. The very next day, He will die for us. By giving His life for us, Jesus recreates our relationship with the Father: a covenant based not on our abilities, choices, or worthiness, but on His love.

Ultimately, the Eucharistic Celebration is intended to be a celebration of love. Jesus, the Son of God, offers His human life so that we can live in true freedom, the freedom of being loved unconditionally. Such an immense love that offers us the greatest freedom begs for a response. So the Mass is not just the renewal of Jesus's sacrifice of love, but also becomes our loving response to His gift of Himself.

The solemn, more formal language that the Church uses in the prayers of the Mass is an effort to express in mere words the inexpressible: the mystery of God's great love and our response.

What has been my response to the immense love Jesus offers me in the Eucharist? How can I participate at Mass more fully, more lovingly? How do I want to live a Eucharistic life from now on?

Take some time to reflect on your personal response to the great gift Jesus makes of Himself to us in the Eucharist.

Pray "Lamb of God . . ." in sorrow for the times you have not been as attentive in celebrating the Eucharist and living a Eucharistic life. Pray also for the grace to center your life on the Eucharist.

Do this in remembrance of me

In Union with Jesus

Jesus asks us to celebrate the Eucharist in His memory. It is not enough just to remember His love. We need to experience His saving love frequently if we are to stay united with Him. When we remain in His love, we bring His love into the world.

Authentic love includes sacrifice, a dying to some of our own desires for the sake of the one we love. The greater the love, the greater the sacrifices we are willing—even happy—to make. If we truly love Jesus, we come to share His interests and desires. And His urgent desire is to bring God's saving love to everyone. He asks of us: "Do *this* in remembrance of me." What does *"this"* mean? Certainly celebrating the memorial of the passion, death and resurrection of Jesus. But couldn't "this" also mean sharing *everything* with Jesus, just as Jesus shares everything with us? Might "this" also mean to give ourselves to others just as selflessly as Jesus gives Himself to us at every Eucharist? His call to us to imitate Him comes just after the institution of the Eucharist in Luke's Gospel: "I am among you as one who serves" (Lk 22:27). In John's Gospel, the washing of the feet is the ultimate symbol of living the Eucharistic life.

"Do this in remembrance of me" is Jesus calling to us to live a Eucharistic life: to share in the life and mission of Jesus, to share in His paschal mystery, to share His love with others.

We might feel overwhelmed by the greatness of this call. Yet the call to live a Eucharistic life is not impossible because Jesus nourishes us with His own Body and Blood. In giving us Himself, Jesus strengthens, comforts, and transforms us. Even though we are weak and sinful, His loving grace can overcome any obstacle. This great mystery of faith is also incredibly personal: in the Eucharistic Celebration, we are transformed into Christ for the world.

We pray for the grace to remain united to Jesus, to center our life on Him, to allow Jesus to transform us. The beautiful prayer below, written by Blessed James Alberione as a thanksgiving after Holy Communion, can be prayed any time for the intention of growing in union with Jesus.

> Pray Saint Paul's Canticle of Love, found in I Corinthians 13:1–14, as a litany. (For example, pray: "Lord Jesus, teach me a love that is patient, that is kind.")

Prayer to Jesus Life after Communion

You may wish to use this prayer as a spiritual communion.

Jesus, my Life, my Joy and
Source of all that is good,
I love You.

Above all, I ask of You that I may love You
and all those redeemed by Your Blood
more and more.

You are the vine and I am the branch:
I want to remain always united to You
so as to bear much fruit.

You are the Font—
pour out an ever greater abundance of grace
to sanctify me.

You are my head, I am Your member:
communicate to me Your Holy
    Spirit with all His gifts.
    May Your kingdom come
    through Mary.

Console and save all those dear
    to me.

Free the souls in purgatory.

Multiply and sanctify those
    called to share in Your
        mission.[3]

Close with a hymn to the Blessed Virgin Mary, such as "Sing of Mary," written by Roland F. Palmer, SSJE, asking for the grace to learn to "live Christ" as she did.

✧ CHAPTER 4 ✧

Blood of Christ, inebriate me

The third petition of the *Anima Christi* prayer invites us to enter fully into the new life of the Paschal Mystery—Jesus's suffering, dying, and rising for us.

"Blood of Christ"

The Church has always had a special devotion to the Precious Blood of Christ, as we know from reading the New Testament:

> You know that you were ransomed from the futile ways inherited from your ancestors, not with perishable things like silver or gold, but with *the precious blood of Christ*, like that of a lamb without defect or blemish. He was destined before the foundation of the world, but was revealed at the end of the ages for your sake. Through him you have come to trust in God, who raised him from the dead and gave him glory, so that your faith and hope are set on God (1 Pet 1:18–21; emphasis added).

Blood is a very powerful symbol of both family and life. Sharing blood means sharing life: to be part of a family. The loss of blood means death. Shedding blood for another is to save and love them in an unparalleled way.

In the Old Testament, the Covenant between God and His Chosen People was celebrated with the blood of animal sacrifices. In the New Covenant, Christ's sacrifice of His life and His very Blood is the only and final sacrifice for our redemption. The passion and death of Jesus on the cross is the definitive expression of all those symbolic meanings of blood—but *transformed* in the light of His resurrection. When we are baptized, we enter into Christ's death and resurrection: we each become a child of God and part of God's family; we are freed from the power of sin and come to life in Christ; and we share in the self-giving love of Jesus, called to extend His reconciliation here on earth to all humanity.

What might have been going on in Jesus's mind and heart when He lost so much blood at the scourging; as He hung on the cross and felt His life and strength drain away? If we listen to the words Jesus spoke at those extreme moments, we discover that Jesus was not engulfed by self-pity, sorrow, loss, or anger. "Father, forgive them." "Father, into your hands I commend my spirit." "It is finished." His thoughts and sentiments, even at these moments of enormous anguish, were about the Father and about saving us.

The Precious Blood of Jesus poured out for us on the cross bridges the gaps of time, earthly sorrows, and doubts that weaken our faith. The Precious Blood of Jesus shed for us is mysterious, stark proof of God's faithful love for us.

———⟡———

Many saints have struggled to express their devotion to the Precious Blood of Jesus. Saint Catherine of Siena meditated so deeply on the passion and death of Jesus that she begins many of her letters with the phrase "in His Precious Blood."

In the Mass, we are invited to enter anew into this shedding of Christ's blood for us. Though Jesus is fully present under both the consecrated bread and wine, the bread and wine are separate and are consecrated separately. This separation is symbolic of the death of Jesus—the separation of His Blood from His Body. It is another reminder of the reality we celebrate in every Eucharist: Jesus offering Himself for our salvation. This petition, *Blood of Christ, inebriate me*, invites us deeper into the mystery of our Redemption.

" . . . inebriate me"

A clue to our spiritual tradition is included in the second part of this petition.

Considering the sacrificial nature of the words "Blood of Christ," wouldn't we expect the invocation to be "save me" or "cleanse me"? Instead, we pray with these unexpected words: "inebriate me." "Inebriate" is a term usually associated with a drunken, stupefied state. When someone is inebriated, they are taken over by alcohol; their behavior changes. When we pray this petition, we are asking to get *drunk* or to be immersed in Jesus. We ask Jesus to flood us with Himself, with His life and love, so that He can take over in us. We ask Jesus to begin or to deepen that process by which we are transformed into Him.

"To be inebriated" is also used to describe being immersed in an experience, for example, inebriated with joy. To be inebriated changes our attitudes and our behavior. In this petition, then, we are clearly not focusing solely on the sorrow we could feel over the passion and death of Jesus. Instead, we are asking for the grace to be immersed and transformed by the Precious Blood of Christ. Bathed and inebriated in the love of Jesus, we can enter more fully into His resurrection, the fullness of life He offers to us. The elation of being loved by God in Christ transforms our vision of ourselves, others, the world, our future, our way of living Christ in the world.

Deep joy is a characteristic of holy people. Saint Francis of Assisi, also known as "God's Jester," was in excruciating pain when he wrote the exuberant "Canticle of the Sun." Martyrs such as Saint Ignatius of Antioch, Saint Lawrence, Saint Isaac Jogues, Blessed Miguel Pro, and countless others amaze us with their joy at the point of death, so immersed are they in the love of Christ. Saints especially known for their charity—such as Blessed Teresa of Calcutta, Saint Philip Neri, and Saint Josephine Bakhita—were admired for their spirit of joyful service.

When we are captivated by Christ's love, we find deep joy. In this petition, we beg Jesus for what He most wants to give us: to allow His transforming love and grace to so fill us that we joyfully *rise* with Him!*

---

* You may use this second part of the chapter to make an hour of adoration by praying with the additional suggestions set apart in the boxes, or you can simply continue reading.

In the Light of God's Word

Uniting ourselves to the Precious Blood of Jesus, we place before the Lord our intentions: to alleviate the sufferings of the world, especially of the innocent victims of violence, war, and oppression. We may wish to pray especially for those who witness to Christ in the face of persecution and threat of death.

Theme for Holy Hour:
Adoring the Victorious Lamb of God

Suggested opening hymn: "Pange Lingua/Tantum Ergo" (written by Saint Thomas Aquinas with various translations into English, such as: "Sing My Tongue the Savior's Glory," translated by Edward Caswall). Spend quiet time in silent adoration.

Adoring Jesus in His Word

Grace to you and peace from him who is and who was and who is to come . . . and from Jesus Christ, the faithful witness, the firstborn of the dead, and the ruler of the kings of the earth.

To him who loves us and freed us from our sins by his blood, and made us to be a kingdom, priests serving his God and Father, to him be glory and dominion forever and ever. Amen.

Look! He is coming with the clouds;
every eye will see him,
even those who pierced him;
and on his account all the tribes of the earth will wail.
So it is to be. Amen.
"I am the Alpha and the
  Omega," says the Lord
  God, who is and who was
  and who is to
come, the Almighty.
(Rev 1:4–8)

Pause for silent reflection either before or after the provided reflection.

Jesus Loves Us

In this reading, we celebrate the victory of Jesus over sin and death. In Baptism, we first receive the fruits of His victory: our true identity as children of God. In the Eucharist, receiving Jesus's Blood strengthens our identity as children of God so that we can *abide* in God's love, in God's life.

Jesus gave Himself completely for us. The Gospel of John offers us a very powerful detail about Jesus's passion, when the soldier pierces the side of Jesus with a lance. Although Jesus had already died, the very last

Images of the Precious Blood of Jesus—beating through His Sacred Heart, running down His sacred body, soaking into the wood of the cross, trickling into the ground—arouse an urgent desire to kiss His sacred wounds, to somehow express our love in return. Shedding one's blood and the giving of one's own life for the sake of another is the most sacred and powerful expression of love—and Jesus did this for us.

drops of His blood pour out from His heart. Jesus saves nothing for Himself, even in death. His blood, like His love, is completely poured out for our sake.

Jesus wants us to receive the full abundance of His love. "I came that they may have life, and have it abundantly" (Jn 10:10). Receiving God's unconditional love changes everything. *We are changed*, at the very core of our being. Even though we still go through all the trials and difficulties of life, we experience them differently. We are no longer tossed about by our sufferings but rooted in the love of the infinite and all-powerful Creator, redeemed from our own sinfulness by the Son of God, and sanctified by the indwelling Spirit. In every experience, no matter how difficult or tragic, we can find comfort, strength, security, and even joy on this sure foundation of God's love. Let us pray for the grace to know and experience always more "the breadth and length and height and depth" of God's love for us in Christ, as Saint Paul describes it (see Eph 3:18–19).

> As an act of faith in Christ's love, pray Saint Paul's prayer in Ephesians (3:16–21).

Jesus Freed Us by His Blood

Following Jesus Way

Jesus could give Himself so completely, so freely, because even while on earth He lived in the Trinitarian communion of love. And He wants us to enter into that same life-giving communion. In becoming a child of God and a brother or sister of Christ, we share in the "riches of His grace," in the fullness of His relationship with the Father and the Spirit.

In every Communion we receive, Jesus invites us to dive into the flood of God's love, allowing Divine Love to flow through us and transform us.

When we receive Jesus in the Eucharist, we are transformed a little more into Him. In one of his medi-

> Pause to thank Jesus for the gift of the Eucharist and for the promise of His love and life in every Communion you have received.

tations, Blessed James Alberione used the comparison of an ill person needing a blood transfusion—as performed in his time—with our need to receive Christ:

> We need a blood transfusion. The vein of the blood donor needs to come in contact with the vein of the person who needs to be strengthened. When those two veins are intimately joined, then

blood will pass from one to the other. The sick and weak person will receive the blood she needs. In the same way, there must be communication, union, between the heart of Jesus and your heart—our heart—so that His divine blood will flow into us until little by little our blood is replaced by His. When this union, this total fusion, between our will and His will takes place, then, to put it briefly, our will is replaced with the will of Jesus; our feelings are replaced with the feelings of Jesus. We live in Jesus—this is love! We are lost in Jesus. It is no longer I who think; it is no longer I who feel; it is no longer I who act. It is Jesus in me! It is Christ who lives in me! You can all make great progress along this path.[1]

What is the fullness or "new life" that I feel God inviting me toward? How have my Communions transformed me into being more Christ-like?

> Use these questions to examine your attitude toward the Eucharist and how you can receive Holy Communion with more fervor.
>
> Pray "Lamb of God . . ." in sorrow for the times you have neglected the Blessed Sacrament.

We can pray:

Blood of Christ, inebriate me. Engulf me in Your love! Transform my selfishness into a self-giving love. Transform my petty concerns into concern for others who do not know You, those who suffer without hope. When I receive You, let the mingling of Your blood with mine change me forever. Through Your Church, sanctified by Your blood, engulf the whole world with Your love!

> You may also want to pray the Litany to the Precious Blood, available in many prayer books and online.

To Him . . . Who Made Us to Be a Kingdom

In Union with Jesus

Our identity as children of God is not static but dynamic; being a child of God is not just who we are but how we live. Ideally, our identity is expressed in all that we do. The Eucharist is the sacrament of love not just because it is one of the highest expressions of Jesus's love for us. The Eucharist is also how Jesus empowers us to live out our identity as children of God in love.

Blood of Christ, inebriate me petitions Jesus for the grace to fully enter this life-giving communion with the Trinity at every Mass. We pray to drink so fully of the love of Jesus in the Eucharist that we will be transformed, sharing in the totality of Christ's self-giving love—His complete and utter letting-go of self.

The Canticle of Ephesians is one of the most expressive prayers of gratitude of the New Testament. Lavish word choices try to capture the inexpressible mystery of our redemption and the unimaginable wealth of being co-heirs with Christ. The Canticle's sumptuous language seeks to express the immensity of the blessings we receive and celebrate at every Eucharistic Banquet of Love. This is a prayer that can become a meditation, each line an opportunity to gratefully marvel at the blessings we receive from the Most Holy Trinity.

Pray this Canticle slowly, phrase by phrase, rejoicing in the many gifts that Jesus gives us in the Eucharist: His presence, His love, His graces, His invitations, His word, His forgiveness, His union with the Father, the beginning of the fulfillment of His promise of eternal life . . .

CANTICLE OF EPHESIANS

Blessed be the God and Father of our Lord Jesus Christ, who has blessed us in Christ with every spiritual blessing in the heavenly places, just as he chose us in Christ before the foundation of the world to be holy and blameless before him in love. He destined us for adoption as his children through Jesus Christ, according to the good pleasure of his will, to the praise of his glorious grace that he freely bestowed on us in the Beloved. In him we have redemption through his blood, the forgiveness of our trespasses, according to the riches of his grace that he lavished on us. With all wisdom and insight he has made known to us the mystery of his will, according to his good pleasure that he set forth in Christ, as a plan for the fullness of time, to gather up all things in him, things in heaven and things on earth. In Christ we have also obtained an inheritance, having been destined according to the purpose of him who accomplishes all things according to his counsel and will, so that we, who were the first to set our hope on Christ, might live for the praise of his glory. (Eph 1:3–12)

Concluding Prayer:
May You be blessed, Jesus Christ, Priest and Sacrifice, Perfect Lamb and worthy Mediator! In You is salvation, resurrection and life. Your blood is the font of salvation: may it rain on me and wash me! Let it fall on the world to purify and save it.[2]

In closing, choose a joyful hymn, such as "We Will Rise Again," composed by David Haas (based on Isaiah 40 and 41), or the traditional "Let All Mortal Flesh Keep Silence," translated by Gerard Moultrie.

⚜ CHAPTER 5 ⚜

Water from the side of Christ, wash me

The fourth petition of the *Anima Christi* prayer focuses on water flowing from the heart of Jesus as a symbol of cleansing and new life—for each of us individually, and for the world.

"Water from the side of Christ"

"But when they came to Jesus and saw that he was already dead, they did not break his legs. Instead, one of the soldiers pierced his side with a spear, and at once blood and water came out" (Jn 19:33–34). The Fathers of the Church saw a great deal of symbolism in the water mixed with blood flowing from the side of Jesus: an image of the sacramental baptismal waters that cleanse us from our sins, and also a reference to the Church, founded on the new life that Jesus came to bring us.

Water is essential for life. We thirst for it, bathe in it, drink it, and wash with it; water nurtures life on our planet. When water is abundant, we take it for granted. But when a big storm threatens, the first thing we do is stock up on water. Without water, our very survival is endangered. And it's not enough to drink a large quantity of water once; we need to drink a certain amount of water every day, usually several times a day, to be healthy.

What water is for our physical survival is akin to what God's grace is for our souls. Without God's grace, we are spiritually trapped in a perilous existence: always thirsting, always dying of drought. When we receive the sacrament of Baptism, we receive the gratuitous gift of God's grace.

Grace is a supernatural gift and a mystery which our Catholic tradition describes in many ways:

✠ sharing in God's own life;

✠ God's favor;

✠ God's help in living our call to holiness.

We can make the mistake of thinking that the grace of our Baptism is something static that happened once—perhaps when we were infants. While it's true that Baptism is received only once and changes us forever, the grace of our Baptism sustains us all our lives. The grace of justification, which we receive in our Baptism, includes the forgiveness of our sins, the gift of our sanctification, and our inner healing and renewal from the effects of sin. Sanctifying grace enables us to respond to our new identity as children of God, to grow in holiness, to fully live our human and Christian vocation to love.

Theological studies and sermons can fool us into thinking of grace as an abstract, generic quality. But grace is anything but generic and abstract. Grace is God's gift of Himself to us. Grace is a sharing of God's life with each of us—the same life that Jesus poured out in blood and water from the cross.

While grace is a supernatural reality, something that can be understood only in the light of faith, its effects in our lives can be felt, often tangibly. Holy people can sometimes seem to facilitate an encounter with grace when we are with them. Certain places of pilgrimage, such as Lourdes, Rome, Guadalupe, and Fatima, are places of grace to the countless pilgrims who visit them.

Love Affair,[1] an overlooked film that deserves to be better known than its popular remake, attempts to show such an encounter with grace. Starring Irene Dunne and Charles Boyer, the heart of this classic love story is not a romantic scene, but a visit that the couple makes to the man's frail grandmother at her peaceful island home.

When they arrive, Irene Dunne's character, Terry, notices something special: "What is there about this place? Something makes you feel you ought to whisper. . . . Such peace. . . ." She makes a visit to the little chapel and prays before a statue of Our Lady of Grace, where she is deeply moved. As Terry leaves the chapel, she finds that she sees everything differently: "I've never seen such lovely colors. Everything seems so vivid. Even the green seems greener." In her conversation with the grandmother, Terry is touched by the wisdom and peace of the tiny, luminous woman, who confides to Terry her fears for her grandson. As she leaves, we sense that Terry's life has changed. She doesn't want to leave—she runs back up the stairs to hug the grandmother, taking strength from the frail woman's inner peace.

Terry has received a tremendous grace: a new vision of life and possibly of her vocation—marriage to the lost and lonely man she has been flirting with. (The spirituality of this scene—which is never explained but is alluded to at key moments in the film—gives the film a depth that its popular remake, *Affair to Remember,*[2] simply does not have.)

Encounters with grace can be small, almost indescribable moments; they can be profound, ground-shaking experiences; or they can be anywhere in between. The key is to be open to God working in us, so that each encounter with grace can transform us, filling us with new life.

To cherish and nurture the mystery of God's life in us, we can:

⚜ thank God for our Baptism and the gift of His life that continues to grow in us, blessing us with joy, peace, and strength;

⚜ deepen our union with God by choosing to spend time in prayer each day, and by receiving the sacraments often;

⚜ pay attention to our choices—big and little—so that our lives can be shaped by grace. This means both avoiding sin and situations that could lead us to sin, and cultivating the virtues we particularly need to grow in Him.

This image of the water that flows from Christ's side, that comes from His Sacred Heart, that is mixed with *His Blood,* that represents the life Jesus sacrificed for us, is a wonderful image for grace, for how God's life intimately transforms us.

" . . . wash me"

"Wash me" is an insistent cry for cleansing, healing, and renewal. We need to be washed from our sinfulness and healed from the wounds we have suffered as a result of our sins and those of others.

"Wash me!" becomes our sincere plea when we know who we are in the sight of God: incredibly beloved and graced, but also indisputably weak and prone to sin. Jesus patiently guides us toward a fuller understanding of ourselves, so that we can rely fully on Him.

Blessed James Alberione received these precious words in a vision of the Eucharist: "Do not be afraid, I am with you. From here (the tabernacle) I will enlighten. Live in continual conversion." These comforting words are inscribed on the walls of every chapel of the Pauline Family around the world. But why would Jesus give that last phrase, "Live in continual conversion," to the young priest who had already made holiness a way of life, and who would share his vision with the Pauline religious priests, brothers, sisters, and consecrated lay people? Because *everyone* needs to live in ongoing conversion. The closer we grow to Christ, the more His brilliance reveals the depths of our shadows, enabling us to see deeper into our own hearts, with all our foibles and woundedness.

Living in continual conversion means more than just avoiding sin and acknowledging our sinfulness when we fail. It means daily recommitment to a life dedicated to Christ. Many saints have joked that our ego dies ten minutes after we do. Their focus on God gave them a greater awareness of human nature—capable of great love and great selfishness, great humility and great pride.

An ordinary and yet marvelous way to experience this sacred cleansing and conversion is to receive the sacrament of Reconciliation. This sacramental encounter with the mercy of Christ is so hard to define that we call the sacrament by many names: Confession, Penance, Reconciliation. An underappreciated gift that the Church continually offers to us, the sacrament of Reconciliation is a way to be healed, renewed, and transformed by God's loving forgiveness. If we are honest with ourselves about our neediness, we will receive this remarkable sacrament more often.

Water from the side of Christ, wash me.

If the chapel you are going to does not have a crucifix easily visible, you may wish to bring a small crucifix or a picture of Jesus Crucified, as well as a copy of the Gospels.*

In the Light of God's Word

Since it was the day of Preparation, the Jews did not want the bodies left on the cross during the Sabbath, especially because that Sabbath was a day of great solemnity. So they asked Pilate to have the legs of the crucified men broken and the bodies removed. Then the soldiers came and broke the legs of the first and of the other who had been crucified with him. But when they came to Jesus and saw that he was already dead, they did not break his legs. Instead, one of the soldiers pierced his side with a spear, and at once blood and water came out. (He who saw

Theme for Holy Hour:

Jesus Crucified

Suggested opening hymn: "O Esca Viatorum," traditional, or "Crown Him with Many Crowns," written by Matthew Bridges and Godfrey Thring.

Ask for the light of the Holy Spirit in listening and praying with God's word. (Suggested prayer/hymn: "Breathe on Me, Breath of God," written by Edwin Hatch, adapted by Anthony G. Petti.)

Adoring Jesus in His Word

You may wish to read this Gospel passage very slowly three times, allowing the words to sink in deeply.

---

* You may use this second part of the chapter to make an hour of adoration by praying with the additional suggestions set apart in the boxes, or you can simply continue reading.

this has testified so that you also may believe. His testimony is true, and he knows that he tells the truth.) These things occurred so that the scripture might be fulfilled, "None of his bones shall be broken." And again another passage of scripture says, "They will look on the one whom they have pierced" (Jn 19:31–37).

These powerful details from an eyewitness draw us in to that moment beneath the cross, standing side by side with Mary, John, and the holy women. In silence, we gaze as Jesus's sacred body is desecrated one more time.

The saints often called the crucifix their *book* which they never stopped reading.

The enormity of what we see—the Son of God dead on the cross, having poured out His life for us—can make us uncomfortable. We might even look away. But we must not let guilt or shame cloud our vision of the crucifixion. Jesus chose to die for us so that our guilt would be washed away in the healing blood and water from His wounded side. Let us receive what Jesus so desperately wants to give us—salvation and the fullness of life.

> Can you imagine standing beneath the cross of Jesus, with Mary, Mary Magdalene, and John?
>
> Which words or phrases in the reading move your heart?

A wise and holy tradition in our Catholic faith places crucifixes everywhere—in our churches and in our homes. "They will look on the one whom they have pierced." *We* are the "they" referred to in the Gospel. But *how* are we to gaze on a crucifix, on this scene of senseless, tragic, unjust violence?

With a gaze that will transform us—a contemplative gaze. A gaze that does not shy away from what we see, a gaze that seeks to understand the gift of love underneath the horror of crucifixion.

> As an act of faith in Jesus's love, renew your baptismal promises. (They can be found in the missal during Easter time.) If you can't find a copy, pray the Nicene Creed.

True contemplation involves two qualities: receptivity and love.

Growing in Contemplation: Receptivity

We gaze on the crucifix, on our crucified Lord, and take in the details that we see. Sometimes it helps to focus on just one detail: the nail in one of His hands, the way His head droops, one thorn, the scrapes on His knees, or perhaps today, at the gaping wound in His side—the wound that leads directly to His heart.

> Allow some time for quiet contemplation of one of the precious wounds of Jesus.

This traditional prayer may help us enter into a spirit of grateful contemplation:

Holy wound in the side of my Jesus, I adore You. I offer You my compassion, O my Jesus, for the cruel insult You suffered. I thank You, my Jesus, for the love which allowed Your side and heart to be pierced, so that the last drops of blood and water might come forth, redeeming me. I offer to the Eternal Father this outrage, and the love of Your most sacred humanity, that my soul may enter once and for all into Your most loving heart, eager and ready to receive the greatest sinners, so that from You I may nevermore depart.

Holy Mother, pierce me through; /In my heart each wound renew/Of my Savior crucified.[3]

We allow the path of that wound to lead us to the Sacred Heart of Jesus. And we remain there, allowing whatever we feel to simply arise, and then we return our gaze back to Jesus, back to His wound of love that heals the world.

Blood and water pour forth from this wound, a "cleansing tide" that has the power to wash away not

Following Jesus Way

just our sins but the sins of the world. The world longs for this cleansing, although it doesn't know it. But we are not unaware. We can receive this cleansing and be freed from the chains of the sinful tendencies that hold us back and hinder us from reaching our full potential. This water does not just wash us, but heals us and draws us closer to the living God. Dare we allow this longing for cleansing and renewal to grow in us?

If we are able to remain still, we will be immersed in the tidal wave of Jesus's love for us—a love that overcomes sin and death.

Alberione wrote, "The life of Jesus is lost through sin. This life has its breath, which is prayer; its nourishment, which is meditation; its sicknesses, which are imperfections and defects; its resource, which is fervor; its joys, which are consolations; its sadnesses, which are desolations; its growth in the saints. . . . Anyone who acts in Jesus Christ is like the branch which partakes in His life, that is, grace: 'He it is that bears much fruit' (Jn 15:5). The life of Jesus Christ is infinite; therefore, the merit and the grace in our heart can grow indefinitely. Let us desire to become saints, and to do so quickly—great saints in Jesus Christ. Let us . . . be in the very heart of Jesus Christ, who immolates Himself upon the altars."[4]

Resting in the heart of Christ, we can ask ourselves:

> We make our examination of conscience, reflecting on these questions, and praying for healing and renewal.

- ❧ What healing do I wish to pray for as I rest in the heart of Jesus?

- ❧ Whom do I want to bring with me into the heart of Jesus to be healed? A loved one? Someone whose need for healing and hope impressed me? Someone I have read about or heard about?

- ❧ How can I "live in continual conversion," allowing the love of Jesus to transform me so that my love and my life truly become like His?

In profound gratitude, we offer our love to the pierced heart of Jesus. Let us fulfill the desire of *His* heart, asking Him to let the blood and water from His heart engulf us, so that, knowing and accepting His

> You may wish to sing or prayerfully read the hymn "Song Over the Waters," composed by Marty Haugen, while praying for healing, forgiveness, and renewal.

saving love more deeply, we can be transformed: freed from fear, freed from selfishness, freed from sin.

We enter the wound in His side and take refuge there, asking for His forgiveness, healing, strength, and perseverance.

Growing in Contemplation: Love

In Union with Jesus

Chapter 17 of the Gospel of John contains the prayer of Jesus to His Father the night before He died. When we read it prayerfully, we find the sentiments with which Christ would offer His life. John 17 is a profound way to contemplate the love of the heart of Christ for us and for the world.

In union with Jesus, pray John 17 for His disciples, for the Church today, for all those who have not yet received the saving love of Christ Jesus. Offer your heart with His for the life of the world.

We remain still, gazing on our Master's pierced side. Later, Jesus will invite Thomas to *put his hand into His side.* We cannot touch the Master's wound with our hands, but we can *touch* His wound with our faith and love, praying this traditional prayer:

PRAYER BEFORE A CRUCIFIX

Good and sweet Jesus, before Your face I humbly kneel and with great fervor of spirit I pray and implore you to instill deep into my heart lively sentiments of faith, hope, charity, true sorrow for my sins, and a firm purpose to amend my life, while I contemplate with great sorrow and love Your five wounds, pondering over them in my mind while remembering the words which David the prophet spoke long ago about You, my Jesus: "They have pierced my hands and my feet; they have numbered all my bones" (Ps 22:16–17).[5]

You can pray this traditional prayer as you conclude the hour of adoration, and also the next time you receive Holy Communion.

Suggested closing hymn: "Alive in Christ Jesus," composed by David Haas (based on Romans 8).

✤ Chapter 6 ✤

Passion of Christ, strengthen me

The fifth petition of the *Anima Christi* prayer focuses on Jesus's passion as our source of strength. We can find this strength especially in the Eucharist, where Jesus renews His saving suffering, death, and resurrection for us and for the world.

"Passion of Christ"

In fulfilling His command at the Last Supper, "Do this in memory of me," the Church continuously celebrates the memorial of Christ's passion and death. At every Mass, the sacrifice of Jesus is made present on our altars for our sake. Yet, it is not uncommon to hear Catholics complain, "I don't get anything out of the Mass." Why this tragic lack of understanding?

✤ Most Catholics have never studied their faith past First Communion or Confirmation instruction. Is it fair to expect a childhood level of understanding to meet adult challenges of faith?

- ⚜ We are not used to seeing with "eyes of faith." Perhaps the way the Eucharist is celebrated is lacking: not reverent enough, distracted, sung poorly, or lacking an engaging homily, etc. Or perhaps suffering has dimmed the light of faith in our lives.

- ⚜ Jesus's passion and death feel irrelevant, distant from our lives, or too uncomfortable to dwell on.

The questions then become: how does the Mass connect with our daily lives? How can we renew our faith and love for the Eucharist, which is the pledge of Christ's self-giving love, the invitation to deeper union with Jesus, and a foretaste or "sneak preview" of heaven? How can we pray with the mystery of Christ's passion, death, and resurrection so that it changes our lives?

As a child, Joan loved to pray with the Stations of the Cross because they made the love of Jesus feel real to her. Later, as Joan grew older, she found she could not enter into the spirit of Lent. Just going to the Palm Sunday Mass and hearing the account of the Lord's passion read aloud brought back memories of a violent trauma she had suffered in her childhood. The thought of Christ's hands nailed to the cross made her relive the memory of her own helplessness and shame. Struggling to find meaning in her tragic past, Joan found herself progressively unable to pray about the central mystery of her faith. After several years, Joan spoke to a wise priest about her spiritual dilemma.

The priest reassured her that she was already sharing in the passion of Christ in her own way, and that it might be more helpful to focus her current prayer on other aspects of God's love—such as praying the psalms, meditating on the miracles and teachings of the public life of Jesus, or reading the Letters of the New Testament that explore how to live the Christian life.

Gradually, as Joan healed from her painful past, she began praying again with the passion, this time taking comfort that Jesus understood her sufferings. Instead of focusing on the physical sufferings of Jesus, her prayer centered on Christ's great love for her, and how she could find meaning in her own sufferings by uniting them with His.

What Joan experienced so intensely, many of us go through in a smaller way. Praying the Stations of the Cross, or meditating on the passion and death of Jesus can be uncomfortable, leading us to feel guilty, to think more about our own suffering or where we have felt disconnected from God's saving love.

But when prayed with sentiments of faith, the passion and death of Jesus can become one of our greatest consolations. "When we look at the crucifix, our primary feeling should not be sadness but rather adoration, contemplation, and gratitude for the salvation that was accomplished in the mystery of life offered on the wood of the cross. On this wood, Christ reigns and draws everyone to Himself, because the cross is the pathway to resurrection."[1]

In addition to learning more about the Eucharist through reading and studies, spending time in adoration outside of Mass is one way we can grow in our appreciation of the Most Holy Sacrament. Blessed James Alberione, whose Pauline spirituality is centered on the Eucharist, made Eucharistic adoration a keystone of Pauline prayer:

"I insist on the Visit [daily hour of adoration], not because it is first. First comes the Mass; second, Communion; and third the Visit; but one who makes adoration well will also make the other two well."[2]

The beauty of the Eucharist is that Jesus comes to be with us in *every* circumstance of our life: the joys, routine, obstacles, sorrows, busyness, sufferings . . . . Jesus does not come to make our lives easy or perfect, but to be with us. His passion strengthens us because we know for certain that we are never alone. Jesus, our Crucified Master, reveals how every moment in our life can have meaning.

When confronted with suffering, we can allow it to embitter us or help us grow: the choice is ours. Jesus gives us the strength to choose growth. Suffering can help us to grow:

- ⚜ by opening our eyes to appreciate what we have, and gifting us with new awareness about what is important in life;

- ⚜ by helping us to recognize and accept our dependence on God;

- ⚜ by making us aware of our interdependence on others;

- ⚜ by increasing our understanding and compassion for the sufferings of others.

Undergoing our own anguish also gives us a very precious opportunity to offer our sufferings in union with Christ's, thus sharing in His mission of salvation for others.

The crucifix is the *icon* that best represents our faith. The Lenten liturgy speaks of the cross as the "Tree of life." When we unite our sufferings to those of Jesus on the cross, we too will experience life—for the passion of Jesus did not end in death but in His resurrection.

" . . . strengthen me"

Because Jesus suffered in every possible way—mentally, physically, emotionally, spiritually—we know that He not only understands our sufferings but can also give us the strength we need in them. Saint Thomas Aquinas highlights three ways the Eucharistic presence of Jesus can offer us strength: Memorial, Banquet, and Presence.

Memorial

Whenever we are tempted to doubt the love of Jesus for us, we only need to glance at a crucifix to remember that His fidelity could never be broken, not even by torture and death.

At every Eucharistic Celebration, Jesus renews His offering of Himself. The gift that Christ makes of His life to the Father for us can be like an earthquake that rocks our lives of routine, forgetfulness, and complacency. His suffering cracks our hard hearts wide open, making space for God's love to enter and become the new foundation of our lives.

In suffering and dying for love of us, Jesus transforms our relationship with suffering and death. For Saint Paul (and for the Church), the suffering and death of Jesus is *always* connected with His resurrection. Jesus died for love of us and to save us from the power of death; Jesus rose to bring us to eternal life. Death itself is changed: no longer is it the end. Rather, death is the beginning of a new, eternal life in Christ where loneliness, suffering, and sin will be no more.

Banquet

In the Eucharistic Celebration, Jesus offers His Body and Blood for us as our food. Just as food taken regularly sustains us physically, so the "Bread of Angels" is meant to be received often, to sustain us and help us grow in union with God, especially in those moments when we are most hurting or needy. The times that we *don't* feel like going to Mass are precisely the times we should not miss going!

At Mass, the Banquet is twofold. The Liturgy of the Word gives us a particular kind of nourishment: God speaks to us in our specific time and circumstance. The carefully chosen readings at Mass can become the source of our prayer and meditation throughout our day or week.

The Liturgy of the Eucharist invites us to enter into and unite ourselves to the offering Jesus makes of Himself to the Father, to be fully present to the renewal of His sacrifice for us, and to receive Him in Holy Communion. Not only does Jesus want us to ask for whatever we need, He wants to give us far more than we in our littleness can imagine. We can ask Him anything and entrust ourselves to Him with utmost confidence.

Speaking of this twofold Banquet, Blessed James Alberione points out that the word of God gives us light for the journey, and Holy Communion gives us the desire and strength to journey on.

Presence

According to Saint Thomas Aquinas, in the Eucharist Jesus humbles Himself even more than in His passion. During His passion, His divinity was hidden, but in the Eucharist His divinity *and*

His humanity are hidden. Just as in the Garden of Gethsemane Jesus desired the company of the apostles, so in the Eucharist Jesus desires our companionship. Yet Jesus in the Blessed Sacrament is often neglected, disrespected, or blasphemed.

Jesus knows what it is to suffer alone, to be misunderstood, rejected, and abandoned by all. Yet He will never let us undergo the depth of His suffering. No matter how alone we feel, Jesus is faithfully present in the Eucharist *for us.* He is our Rock and faithful Friend to lean on, our Harbor in whom we can rest safely, the Shepherd who never leaves our side. In being physically with us in His real Eucharistic presence, Jesus offers us a tangible, physical closeness. In faith our senses reach out in adoration: we adore Him with our gaze lit by faith, we kneel before Him in adoration, we cradle Him in our hands as we receive Communion, we taste the reality of His love. Whatever strength we need, when we encounter Jesus in the Eucharist, we can lean on His merciful love and unshakable fidelity. Jesus will never abandon us.*

In the Light of God's Word

Theme for Holy Hour:

Praying with Jesus on the Cross

When it was noon, darkness came over the whole land until three in the afternoon. At three o'clock Jesus cried out with a loud voice, "Eloi, Eloi, lema sabachthani?" which means, "My God, my God, why have you forsaken me?"

---

* You may use this second part of the chapter to make an hour of adoration by praying with the additional suggestions set apart in the boxes, or you can simply continue reading. Along with your Bible, bring a copy of the Stations of the Cross to pray with during this hour.

When some of the bystanders heard it, they said, "Listen, he is calling for Elijah." And someone ran, filled a sponge with sour wine, put it on a stick, and gave it to him to drink, saying, "Wait, let us see whether Elijah will come to take him down." Then Jesus gave a loud cry and breathed his last. And the curtain of the temple was torn in two, from top to bottom. Now when the centurion, who stood facing him, saw that in this way he breathed his last, he said, "Truly this man was God's Son!" (Mk 15:33–39)

Suggested opening hymn: "When I Survey the Wondrous Cross," written by Isaac Watts.

Adoring Jesus in His Word

The words of Jesus in this Gospel, "My God, my God, why have you forsaken me?" can shock us. If Jesus is truly the Son of God, wouldn't He have known with certainty that the Father would not abandon Him?

As Son of God, Jesus knows the Father better than we ever could—including His infinite goodness and love. But knowing something and feeling something are two different things. On the cross, Jesus took on all that we suffer, including the sense of separation from God that sin brings. His desolate cry, asking the Father why He had abandoned Him, is also an act of faith because Jesus is quoting Psalm 22. In this psalm, every time the psalmist complains about suffering, he follows it with a remembrance of how the Lord has cared for him. Psalm 22 ends with a hymn glorifying and praising God's goodness and deliverance.

What does it mean to us that the suffering of Jesus is both akin to ours and goes way beyond it? As man, Jesus fully undergoes not just the physical aspects of suffering, but also the hostility and rejection of the very people He came to save. As Son of God, Jesus takes on the devastating evil of sin—the hell of separation from God—more than any mere human being could bear. It wasn't enough for Him to suffer for us and with us. Jesus wanted to take on the full consequences of sin, to definitively free us from the power of sin and death. He undergoes a senseless, horrific death where He experiences utter desolation so that we will not have to experience the ultimate, eternal suffering of separation from God.

In union with Jesus on the cross, renew your trust in God's love for you and God's plan for your life by praying Psalm 22.
Try to bring the *rhythm* of this psalm into daily life: every time you complain about something, turn it into a prayer of faith and/or praise.

We will never comprehend the depth of Christ's suffering or the depth of His love for us.

In our lives, profound suffering usually involves our entire being; if we are physically suffering, we find

Following Jesus Way

ourselves emotionally and spiritually dry. Psychological suffering often leads to physical illness. However we suffer, we tend to feel isolated, fragmented, and disconnected from others and from God. Unable to see meaning or hope at the time when we most need to, our suffering becomes even more painful, tinged with our desperation and hopelessness.

During His passion, Jesus experienced that fragmentation and hopelessness too. Because He fully, freely, and lovingly suffered His passion and cross to bring us to new life, we can glimpse the resurrection even in our present sufferings. It is not just that our sufferings will not last forever. Rather, our suffering is *infused* with the hope of the resurrection, with the certainty that we are accompanied and loved, with the conviction that whatever we undergo will somehow bring new life—even if we cannot see it now. For when we unite our sufferings with those of Jesus, they become a source of life for others. Just as the centurion saw God's holiness in Christ's death on the cross, so our sufferings can become an opening for God's grace to enter the world.

In this way, we suffer and die with Christ in order to rise with Him.

"Faith creates in us a new being, animated by the spirit of Jesus Christ. United with Him, abandoned in Him in this life, we *can* accomplish and we *do* accomplish what He did: in Him we die to the flesh and to sin, to be born again into the spiritual life. Speaking more precisely: Christ alone lives, thinks, acts, loves, wills, prays, suffers, dies, and rises in us."[3]

Perhaps we can reflect on these questions: How am I living the paschal mystery in my daily life? What am I going through right now that feels like an obstacle to my life of faith? What can strengthen me to unite both my joys and my sufferings with Jesus?

We can renew our love for Jesus Crucified with this prayer for union with Him:

CRUCIFIED WITH CHRIST

May Your unchanging patience be my patience.

May Your crown of thorns obtain for me humility of heart.

May Your scourging be my purity and mortification.

May Your agony be the model of my agony.

May the wounds of Your holy feet guide all my footsteps.

May the folly of Your cross give me true wisdom.

May Your resurrection obtain for me a glorious resurrection.

In all things may I be crucified with You, and may Your holy will be entirely fulfilled in me.

May Your merits be mine, and Your virtues be for me way, strength, mercy, and eternal reward.[4]

— Blessed James Alberione

To continue your contemplation, pray the Stations of the Cross with the intention of asking for the strength to live your entire life —including the challenges and sufferings—in union with Jesus. You may wish to include in your intentions someone else who is undergoing great suffering.

In Union with Jesus

Conclude with a hymn of praise for the gift of our redemption in Christ, such as the traditional "What Wondrous Love Is This."

CHAPTER 7

O Good Jesus, hear me

The sixth petition of the *Anima Christi* prayer is a simple plea expressing the urgency of our prayerful desires—springing from our hearts directly to the heart of Jesus.

"Good Jesus"

Names are important. Entire books are dedicated to helping writers choose the best name for their fictional characters.

The names we use for God can reveal a lot about our relationship with God: our image of God, how close we feel to God, and our trust (or lack of trust) in Him. We naturally pray with names of God that are familiar and intuitively appealing, but we can also choose to pray with a particular name or title of God. Regularly using a specific name for God or Christ can then shape our prayer life.

"Good Jesus" begins another intimate petition of the *Soul of Christ* prayer. Calling Jesus "good" is a beautiful act of faith in His goodness—in His divine, loving nature and His saving will for our greatest good and eternal happiness.

The name *Jesus* comes from the Hebrew language and means "God saves." One of the simplest but also most profound prayers is to simply speak the name of Jesus. In His name, we acknowledge the entirety of salvation history and most specifically our redemption. As a prayer, *Jesus* is:

- ⚜ an act of faith: we express our faith in Jesus as our all-powerful God and loving Savior;

- ⚜ an act of hope: a plea for Jesus to save us anew today;

- ⚜ an act of love and gratitude: an honest acknowledgment that our lives have been transformed by His love;

- ⚜ an act of adoration: that the Son of God would take on human nature and a human name in order to save us.

When we call Jesus by name in our prayer, what are our thoughts and sentiments behind this one word?

" . . . hear me"

By plainly saying the words, *hear me*, we express our trust that Jesus will do so. How awesome it is to know that we have a God who bends over us, who would strain to hear our whispered pleas if needed. But God's hearing is perfect—especially with regard to those whom He loves.

What can we do when our prayer is dry, when we feel that our spirits are lifeless, when our faith has been tested for so long that we fear its fragile thread will break? How do we respond to our doubts that, if God loves us, He would not let our prayers go unanswered?

The short answer is that God *always* answers our prayers, but often not in the way or time we expect. Blessed James Alberione puts it this way: "Prayer will obtain either what it asks for or something even better."[1]

The petition *Good Jesus, hear me* reminds us to bring to Jesus what we truly desire. Our deepest desires are an important part of who we are and thus important in our relationship with Christ. A deep desire is more than a superficial want or passing whim. Our deeper longings shape us; they express our nature and our gifts from God; they can reflect the working of the Spirit within us, leading us on our unique spiritual journey.

But because we have to struggle against the woundedness of our nature, we can often confuse our deep desires with sinful inclinations or passions. Both strongly engage our feelings. Discernment is important in helping us to discover which of our desires are indeed gifts from God and which are not. It can be so confusing that at times, we might consider it virtuous to ignore or discount all our longings. But if a desire is a gift from God and an indication of God's will, simply ignoring it could lead us to miss out on something important.

When I was a teenager, I had many dreams for the future. But when I entered the convent, I assumed that I should give them all up, including a childhood dream to write.

Fast-forward five years. I started to understand that in creating me, God had gifted me with specific abilities and limitations. The more I prayed about it, the more it seemed God wanted me to actively use this unique combination of gifts and limitations He had given me for His service. As my desire to write grew, I hesitantly started journaling. At first it felt a bit selfish, because it was something I *wanted* to do. But as my joy and skill in writing deepened, I continually asked Jesus to lead me. Ten years later, I published my first book about Eucharistic adoration. Writing is now a part of my mission as a Pauline sister, as well as a special blessing that enriches my life. It is a gift God places in me, and my desire to write gives me the courage to use that gift.

When we pray with our deep desires, our prayer can surprise us with its joy, insight, and liveliness. God wants our greatest happiness and joy; God delights in fulfilling our deep desires—desires that He has often planted in us. Entrusting our longings to God allows God to work more freely in us and to bring them to bear fruit in God's time and way.

God gives us certain desires because they will lead us to fulfill our mission and draw us closer to Him. But the context of the prayer *Anima Christi* directs us to the most important desire that we can bring to God: a desire for holiness. Each petition is shot through with this longing for union with God. In the context of the rest of the prayer, "Good Jesus, hear me!" expresses the urgency of our need for holiness and transformation in Christ.*

In the Light of God's Word

We know that the whole creation has been groaning in labor pains until now; and not only the creation, but we ourselves, who have the first fruits of the Spirit, groan inwardly while we wait for adop-

Theme for Holy Hour:
Praying in Our Weakness

Suggested opening hymn: "Nearer Than Before," by Jim Cowan.

Begin your hour of adoration by placing before Jesus your deep desires.

Adoring Jesus in His Word

---

* You may use this second part of the chapter to make an hour of adoration by praying with the additional suggestions set apart in the boxes, or you can simply continue reading.

tion, the redemption of our bodies. For in hope we were saved. Now hope that is seen is not hope. For who hopes for what is seen? But if we hope for what we do not see, we wait for it with patience. Likewise the Spirit helps us in our weakness; for we do not know how to pray as we ought, but that very Spirit intercedes with sighs too deep for words. And God, who searches the heart, knows what is the mind of the Spirit, because the Spirit intercedes for the saints according to the will of God. We know that

all things work together for good for those who love God, who are called according to his purpose (Rom 8:22–28).

Pause for reflection.

When we are groaning or waiting for answers, we experience the *not yet* paradox of the Christian life. In faith we believe that we have been saved, but we do "not yet" experience the fullness of redemption while we live on earth. We still suffer, experience temptations, and struggle to consistently act lovingly and justly in a world marred with selfishness and injustice.

Chapter eight of Saint Paul's Letter to the Romans invites us to pray with our deep desires—desires that are too profound to put into words—in the heart of the Trinity. This passage also offers some guidance for when we face obstacles or dryness in our prayer.

We can completely trust in the God who loves us. The times when our prayers seem unanswered, our souls feel dry, and our hearts are desperate are the most fruitful moments to renew our trust.

Share our desires with our loving Father

When we feel our prayers are going unanswered, we can share our hopes and disappointments with God. Holding back what we really think or feel is never good for a relationship. Sharing our deepest desires—our moments of hope, pain, and joy—leads to a special intimacy. God knows our desires already—Saint Paul reminds us that God knows us better than we know ourselves. But daring to entrust our deepest desires to God in prayer is a fruitful practice.

- ❧ We get to know ourselves better, acknowledging how important this desire is to us.

- ❧ We grow in trust in God, to whom we entrust the desire.

- ❧ In giving our desire to God, the desire itself is often changed. Perhaps for the first time, our desire is placed in its true context—the context of God's loving plan for us. It loses its absolute value and becomes as important as it is meant to be.

- ❧ We acknowledge our dependence on our loving Creator and have the opportunity to turn with real hope to the all-powerful One who loves us.

Blessed James Alberione offers this wise advice: "Tell Jesus everything; if you have some troubles, if your heart is full of hope, full of the desire to be united with him . . . . Confide even those worries that you dare not say to anyone . . . tell him even if your shoe hurts. Tell Jesus everything, with the simplicity of a child."[2]

ACT OF TRUST

Jesus, You are my Savior and the Center of my life; I trust completely

As your act of faith, share openly with the Lord all your hopes, troubles, and fears, expressing your trust in His care for you, perhaps in the words of this prayer. When you have poured out your heart, pray the Our Father.

in Your saving love at work in my life right now and for all eternity; I love You who are Love with my whole being! I adore You as my Lord who humbled Himself to undertake the salvation of the world for love of me and for love of every human person.

Imitate Jesus in His Trust in the Father

Following Jesus Way

One of the more puzzling parables is that of the wicked judge who is hounded by the widow to rule in her favor (see Lk 18:1–8). This parable—along with other sayings of Jesus—highlights the importance that Jesus gives to perseverance in prayer. Jesus, who knows human nature by personal experience, reveals how important perseverance is in the spiritual life, in prayer, in our relationships. But perseverance is hard for us who live in a culture where instant gratification seems almost a necessity. The neglected virtues of patience, perseverance, commitment, and endurance are all related to growing in trust. To truly grow in trust, we must be *unable* to see and understand the workings of God.

Jesus gives us a very personal example of perseverance in prayer. The night before He died in the Garden of Gethsemane, Jesus prayed three times to His Father that He would not have to undergo His passion . . . and three times He resolved His heartbroken plea by surrendering to the Father, "Your will be done" (Mt 26:42).

You may wish to read Matthew 26:36–46 and pray with Christ's words to the Father.

⸺◦⟨๑⟩◦⸺

As human beings, we grow through trial and error, through practice and perseverance. We are called to pray regularly, frequently, and not just when we want something. Blessed James Alberione encourages us to pray with an understanding of our desires but also with trust:

> Prayer is necessary in the plan of Divine Providence, since without special divine help we cannot practice certain virtues, fulfill certain duties, overcome certain passions, and persevere for a long time in doing good. Only to one who prays is such help given. . . . Prayer will obtain either what it asks for or something even better.[3]

⚜ What are the patterns of my prayer?

⚜ How do I regularly express my deep desires to Jesus?

⚜ How do I want to grow in my trust of my loving Lord?

Using these questions, reflect on your part in your relationship with Jesus, on your prayer time and how you pray throughout each day.

We can use the very blindness of our faith and our inability to hear God's response to our prayer to grow in trust, clinging to the promise of His love. "Now hope that is seen is not hope" (Rom 8:24). Only in

Renew your trust and spirit of prayer by praying Psalms 62 and 131, psalms that Jesus must have prayed during His earthly life.

heaven will we understand the mysterious ways that God works in our lives and in the world. But we can begin to trust God more fully today.

Pray in the Spirit

In Union with Jesus Life

When God is silent, our prayer not only seems fruitless and dry, but painful. We become raw, or supersensitive to the doubts that silence engenders. But this is not a time to give space to doubts that question God's goodness or our own lovability. We might find it helpful to voice our doubts or write them down, and then dismiss them by tearing them up. If a doubt is persistent or particularly difficult to confront we can look for a Scripture passage that contradicts that doubt, and then spend some time with that particular passage, allowing the word of God to sink deeply into our minds and hearts.

> If you would like, try this during your adoration. Write down a doubt you have, then find a Scripture passage that dispels it. Pray slowly with this one passage.

We may experience sufferings that are beyond words, which we cannot express or articulate. This is a time to simply breathe in God's presence. It can be very powerful to simply sit still in a Eucharistic chapel and allow the warmth of Jesus's presence to comfort us. It is not easy to live these words from Romans 8—to offer the sighs of our spirit to the Holy Spirit, believing that He

> Deepen your adoration and trust of the Most Holy Trinity by praying the "Veni Creator Spiritus" in one of its versions. (This prayer is the basis for the words of the hymn, "Come, Holy Ghost.") Or pray your own Litany to the Holy Spirit, spontaneously using names that come to mind such as: Spirit of truth, enlighten me; Spirit of mercy, gentle my heart, etc.

breathes in us, works in us, and wraps us in the Father's embrace—when we cannot feel Him with us. What we can do is cling to the conviction that, whether we feel comforted or not, "all things work together for good for those who love God, who are called according to his purpose" (Rom 8:28).

These "holy groanings" of our spirit, offered in Jesus's Spirit to the Father, may be a prayer that transforms the world.

You can conclude your adoration with a hymn such as: "Envía Tu Espíritu" ("Send Out Your Spirit"), composed by Bob Hurd (based on Psalm 104 and the Sequence of Pentecost).

⚜ Chapter 8 ⚜

Within Your wounds, hide me

The seventh petition of the *Anima Christi* prayer is a cry for refuge and connects deeply to the next two petitions. All of us have moments in our lives when we need strength and encouragement to confront evil, to persevere through the challenges of discipleship, and to love selflessly. Who better to go to than Jesus, wounded for love of us?

"Within your wounds"

Meditating on the wounds Jesus suffered for us is a way we can take refuge in God's love. In moments of weakness, temptation, and frailty, we have one safe place we can turn to: the heart of Jesus. Jesus opens his heart to us unconditionally, with no limits. If we need proof of His love for us, we simply need to sit in front of a crucifix and meditate on the wound in His side, pierced through by a lance to His Sacred Heart.

While most of us prefer to acknowledge only our strengths, the wounds of Jesus remind us that for our sake, the Son of God took on the weaknesses inherent in our human condition and embraced them fully. Saint Paul learned to rejoice in his weaknesses because they compelled him to rely on Christ rather than on himself.

A young man suffered a terrible betrayal and was unable to let go of the injury or forgive. His anger at the injustice and cruel betrayal haunted him. He knew he was supposed to forgive, but couldn't. Every time he heard a homily about forgiveness, he felt ashamed that he wasn't strong enough to just get past what happened.

He confided his situation and sense of feeling trapped to a priest in confession. The priest told the young man that forgiveness would help him to move forward, but that, because of the deep injustice and betrayal involved, he shouldn't try to force it. "I don't want to forgive," blurted the young man. "I just want to forget about what happened!"

"And yet, you brought it to confession," the priest said. "This is a big step. You've admitted that on your own, you cannot forgive your betrayer. Now is the time to bring to God both your anger and your inability to forgive," the priest advised. "And if you're not ready to ask for the grace to forgive, just ask God for the desire to forgive someday."

After his confession, the young man was finally able to admit his inability to forgive. As he let go of his shame and prayed for the desire to forgive, he gained a sense of peace. It took time, but eventually the young man received the grace to forgive, and he has since moved forward with his life.

———⋯⊙⊙⋯———

When we don't acknowledge our faults and weaknesses out of shame or fear, we can give into a false pride. If we hide our weaknesses from others, we can be tempted to hide them from ourselves, too, thus distorting our self-knowledge and limiting our ability to grow. Blind to our weaknesses, we cannot take them into account. We can be harsh and judgmental of the faults of others because we are unaware of our own. Pushed underground, a fault becomes an invisible force that can sabotage our best efforts.

How often we allow shame for our weaknesses to drive us away from Christ! We forget that the Son of God fully experienced what it means to be human, and that God knows all about our limitations and weaknesses. Those times when we feel weakest, instead of just pretending to others or ourselves that everything is fine, we can confide in our Savior. One of the greatest gifts of our faith is that Jesus is truly human and truly divine, and that He wants a relationship with us. Can we take advantage of this great gift—the desire of Jesus to be close to us—when we find ourselves struggling with our weakness? Instead of running away in shame or shattered pride, the wise spiritual choice is to turn *to* Jesus to share our weakness and sinfulness with Him, so that He can heal, comfort, and strengthen us.

" . . . hide me"

It requires a special kind of strength to share our vulnerability—even with our God who knows our weaknesses better than we do. Yet in the Gospels, Jesus never turns down someone who comes to him with this kind of honesty. The "miracle within a miracle" accounts of Jairus and the woman with a hemorrhage (see Lk 8:43–48; Mt 9:18–26; Mk 5:21–43) are powerful stories of a man and a woman desperately reaching out to Jesus for healing. The woman with a hemorrhage was extremely vulnerable; even touching the cloak of Jesus in her physical condition was forbidden. But Jesus understands her vulnerability and her faith, and instantly heals her. The synagogue leader, Jairus, is a father desperate to save his daughter. He acknowledges his helplessness and begs Jesus to heal her. When friends arrive with the news that she has already died, Jesus does not hesitate. He responds to the father's honest, anguished plea by raising his daughter from the dead—a rare miracle for Jesus.

A visitor asked a young boy what school he attended. "Secret Heart School," was the boy's response.

Have we unintentionally made Jesus's heart one of the biggest "secrets" of our faith? In our daily lives, how often do we worry about being judged by God; and how often do we rejoice in God's love for us?

If we knew that the heart of Jesus, wounded for love of us, was always available for a hidden, one-on-One encounter, would we "hide" in His heart? In the Sacred Heart of Jesus, we are completely safe, accepted for who we are, embraced by His unconditional love, renewed by His delight in us.

Contemplating Christ's wounds can heal us

When we share our neediness with Jesus, we become more receptive to the strength and comfort He wants to give us. We can reach out for His healing grace when . . .

- ✠ temptations lure us;
- ✠ the needs of our ego overwhelm us with selfish desires, the need for security, or the desire for instant gratification;
- ✠ the world's gaze—whether full of praise, contempt, or indifference—distracts us from what is truly important;
- ✠ we fear the future;
- ✠ we are burdened by pain or anxiety for a loved one.

We need and pray for all kinds of healing, but Jesus wants to heal us most from sin. The sins of the world have de-formed our lives and our relationships; our own sinful choices have hurt others, but most deeply, our sins have wounded us.

The wounds of Jesus remind us that, like us, Christ experienced the consequences of sin. But in His resurrection, Jesus has overcome sin and death in all its forms. Because He became vulnerable for us, we can find the courage to approach Jesus and be healed. The wounds that Jesus carries on His risen body—the nail marks on His hands and feet, and His pierced side—are healing for us (see Is 53:5). Jesus underwent a horrific death and rose again not just to share our experience, but also to transform all suffering and death into something life-giving.

Within your wounds, hide me is a prayer that acknowledges that Jesus was wounded for love of us; those wounds reveal how much Jesus wants to be close to us. At first glance the wounds of Jesus are reminders of His death, but when we pray with them, they become much more:

- ✠ proof of Jesus's resurrection;
- ✠ proof of His vulnerability—of His truly taking on our human limits—in His desire to be close to us;

⚜ proof of His constant and saving love for us.

In addition to comforting and healing us, Jesus also wants to send us into the world with the gifts of faith, hope, and love. With clearer self-knowledge, a firm intent to live God's will, and the conviction that we are not alone but embraced in love, we return to our situation to find our circumstances transformed, full of possibility. Or perhaps we will find that it is we who have changed.

The truth is that the whole world is treasured in the heart of Christ. But sometimes, only by seeking refuge in Him are we able to see the possibilities in the tragic and difficult circumstances that we face.*

In the Light of God's Word

Theme for Holy Hour:

Contemplating the Healing Wounds of Christ

But Thomas (who was called the Twin), one of the twelve, was not with them when Jesus came. So the other disciples told him, "We have seen the Lord." But he said to them, "Unless I see the mark of the nails in his hands, and put my finger in the mark of the nails and my hand in his side, I will not believe."

A week later his disciples were again in the house, and Thomas was with them. Although the doors were shut, Jesus came and stood among them and said, "Peace be with you." Then he said to Thomas, "Put your finger here and see my hands. Reach out your hand and

---

* You may use this second part of the chapter to make an hour of adoration by praying with the additional suggestions set apart in the boxes, or you can simply continue reading.

put it in my side. Do not doubt but believe." Thomas answered him, "My Lord and my God!" Jesus said to him, "Have you believed because you have seen me? Blessed are those who have not seen and yet have come to believe." (Jn 20:24–29)

Suggested opening hymn: "Lord Jesus, When I Think of Thee," written by Richard Rolle, or "O Sacred Head Surrounded," attributed to Saint Bernard of Clairvaux, translated by H. Baker.

Begin with an act of adoration of the Sacred Heart of Jesus.

Adoring Jesus in His Word

Why wouldn't Thomas believe that the other disciples had seen the Lord? We can guess at the reasons. Earlier, Thomas had proposed going to die with Jesus (see Jn 11:16). But his heart and his hopes must have been cruelly crushed by the crucifixion. Like the other disciples, he couldn't imagine the possibility of the resurrection. (The other apostles didn't believe Mary Magdalene when she told them she had seen the Risen Lord.) Perhaps Thomas had been so devas-

After reading the Scripture and reflection, bring your wounds—physical, emotional, and spiritual— to Jesus.

tated by the passion and death of Jesus that he simply pushed away everyone he was close to; he was afraid to hope, to feel anything at all.

Whatever his reasons, Thomas stood in the ruins of shattered hopes and demolished faith—as many of us have. We can find hope and healing when we respond to Christ's invitation to enter into His wounds, contemplate His love, and allow that love to be our defense, our healing, our hope.

Pray for the gift of God's healing love with the words of Psalm 103:1–13.

The Gospel of John does not tell us if Thomas actually probed the wounds with his fingertips. Perhaps

it was enough for Thomas to see Jesus. But Jesus invites us to enter into His wounds, take refuge in them, contemplate them, even hide in them. Why would we need to hide, and what are we hiding from?

Hiding in Christ's Wounds Can Bring Healing

We might need to take refuge in the wounds of Jesus simply because we are weak and do not feel ready for the difficulties confronting us. "Hiding" in Christ gives us the space and strength to honestly acknowledge our weaknesses in the safety of God's love. "Hiding" in Jesus gives Him the opportunity to begin healing the deep roots of sin in us. Jesus may heal us quickly or gradually, but if we give Him the space to work within us, He can transform our weaknesses into doorways for His grace.

Hiding in Christ's Wounds Brings New Perspective

"Hiding" can give us a break from the crazy pressures of the world, with its distorted views, expectations, and lack of faith. In Christ, we can rediscover a perspective of faith. Faith gives priority to what is truly important in our lives—for example, not a better salary, but a more loving family; not more prestige or a higher position, but a more selfless service of others. The perspective that comes when contemplating Christ's sufferings can help us to see our circumstances with new eyes.

Hiding in the Wounds of Jesus Brings Strength and Companionship

If we need to hide because we are suffering or afraid, Christ's wounds remind us how much He suffered for love of us, and that He will never allow us to suffer alone. A faithful companion in our suffering can transform what seems unendurable into the greatest gift of love.

When we are in a situation with an uncertain outcome, there is nothing like being able to count on a teammate "to have our back." *That* is what the wounds of Jesus tell us. At our most desperate, Jesus "has our back." He will never desert us, He will always be with us.

Blessed James Alberione once said, "Every pain confided to Jesus becomes light; if accepted from His hands, it ceases to be a cross."[1] What in my life have I kept apart from Jesus, not confiding in Him? Can I entrust it to Him now? How can His touch heal me and transform my struggle to become life-giving?

As the death of Jesus brought about His resurrection, when we hide in the wounds of Jesus, we discover that Jesus wants to transform *our* wounds. What can they then become?

As you ponder your struggles from the new perspective of the pierced heart of Jesus, offer them to the Father with Jesus on the cross.

Make an act of trust by offering the wound you struggle with most—whether a weakness, sinfulness, suffering, or circumstance—and ask Jesus to transform it into something life-giving for you and for others.

Take a few moments to thank the Lord for the gift that your woundedness can become for you and for others.

We can unite ourselves with Jesus in a special way by praying Eucharistically. In the Eucharist, Jesus reveals His vulnerability by risking abandonment, contempt, and sacrilege to be close to us. Jesus takes this risk because He wants us

In Union with Jesus

"By means of the cross, souls receive the life of grace, the Church receives power, and every blessing descends."[2]

to come to Him in our weakness—when we are discouraged, hopeless, overwhelmed, or grief-stricken. When we take refuge in Christ's vulnerable Eucharistic presence, we are "hiding in His wounds" in a particular way. In our Eucharistic visits, Jesus invites us to pray for the gift of renewal and transformation, so that His wounds may transform ours into something glorious.

We can pray the sorrowful mysteries of the Rosary, asking Mary, who most closely accompanied Jesus in His passion, death, and resurrection, to help us enter more deeply into the paschal mystery, so that our sufferings may be transformed into opportunities for grace.

Heart of Jesus, pierced with a lance, have mercy on us.
Heart of Jesus, source of all consolation, have mercy on us.
Heart of Jesus, our life and resurrection, have mercy on us.
Heart of Jesus, our peace and reconciliation, have mercy on us.
Heart of Jesus, salvation of those who hope in You, have mercy on us.

As a closing prayer, you may wish to pray the full Litany to the Sacred Heart of Jesus (found in many prayer books or online).

Suggested closing hymn: "Stabat Mater" ("At the Cross Her Station Keeping"), attributed to Jacopone da Todi, translated by Edward Caswall.

CHAPTER 9

Permit me not to be separated from You

The eighth petition of the *Soul of Christ* is worded negatively but brings us back to the prayer's overall theme, expressing the goal of our entire spiritual lives: union with Christ.

"Permit me not to be separated from You"

I used to think this poetically phrased petition had been put in the wrong place, coming way too late in the prayer. We've already prayed to be sanctified, saved, cleansed, and strengthened. Doesn't all of that presume that we are already united with Christ?

But the placing of this petition so late in the prayer reminds us that spiritual vigilance and continual commitment to conversion are crucial to discipleship—no matter where we are on our spiritual journey. It prompts us to ask important questions, such as: What do we allow to come between Jesus and us? What "separates" us from a deeper union with Christ?

The only thing that can truly separate us from God is sin, as many of the saints have shown us.

Blessed Zdenka Schelingová was a Sister of Charity of the Holy Cross serving as a nurse when the Communist regime took control in Slovakia in 1948. As the regime started persecuting the Catholic Church, Sister Zdenka courageously sought to ease the sufferings of the persecuted priests who came under her care, even helping them escape. But she was finally caught for such an attempt in 1952. Accused of treason, she was interrogated and brutally tortured by the police. She was finally sentenced to prison with no civil rights. The severe beatings and torture that mutilated her body, along with the inhumane conditions of her imprisonment, destroyed her health. In one cell, she used her shoes for a pillow. In another, she faced starvation. Another prison was so bleak and dark that a visitor described it as "terrifying."

Finally after three years Sister Zdenka was released, so that the government would not be blamed for her death. She died three months later, thirty-eight years old, after receiving the immense comfort of Holy Communion.

Despite tremendous physical sufferings during her imprisonment—often in solitary confinement—Blessed Zdenka suffered most from being deprived of the sacraments. Yet those who met her, even when she was in prison, testify to her peace of spirit. On her deathbed, her prayer was for God's mercy. Beatified by Saint John Paul II in 2003, she is considered a martyr; not even death could separate her from God's loving mercy.

❖❖❖

Sin as Separation from God

When we sin, we jeopardize our relationship with God. Spiritually, we turn our hearts away from God. In the case of venial—that is, less serious—sin, we weaken our relationship with God. Repeated and deliberate venial sins make it easier for us to commit more sins.

In the case of mortal sin, where our sinful choice is deliberate, free, and of a serious nature, we choose to break off our relationship with God, turning completely away from Him. Mortal sin is a fundamental disconnect from ourselves, from others, and from God; we no longer share in God's life. Our life and relationship with God can be restored by a deep sorrow for sin and the sacrament of Reconciliation.

Although sin violates our very nature as persons, revulsion for sin is no longer intuitive today. We have lost a sense of the consequences of sin, perhaps because we live in a culture which hoists narcissism onto a pedestal and crushes faith into near-invisibility. Created for love, goodness, and beauty, we allow sin to substitute illusions for reality. Ultimately, sin is a betrayal of who we are: it corrupts our God-given nature and purpose to love, misdirecting us away from our God-given destiny of eternal happiness.

The sacraments are the ordinary way that Jesus gives us to overcome the power of sin in our lives. Receiving the sacrament of Penance not only restores our relationship with God if we have sinned mortally, but, when received frequently, can heal us and help us form a healthy conscience, resist our tendency to sin, and grow in grace. However, it is receiving the Eucharist worthily—after the sacrament of Penance if we have committed mortal sin—that most deeply nurtures our union with God. In receiving Holy Communion, we receive Jesus Himself, whose gift as Love Himself revivifies our own love and strengthens us against sin with the gift of His friendship.

A Spiritual Perspective on the Struggle with Sin

As followers of Christ, we seek to overcome our sinful tendencies and, as much as possible, to avoid sin and temptation. Because of this fervent desire, we can put undue emphasis on the number of times we overcome temptation, or the sins that we do not commit, rather than on God's unrelenting desire—and action—to save us.

Instead, the word of God reminds us to nurture a genuine spiritual perspective when it comes to our own struggle with sin. First, it is beneficial to focus more on our attitudes and disposition than on results. Grand gestures are less impressive to God than an attitude of conversion: "The sacrifice acceptable to God is a broken spirit; a broken and contrite heart" (Ps 51:17). One of the dangers for those who seek to live spiritually is a tendency toward *proving* our holiness, or *counting* our victories over temptation. Our need for reassurance that we are on the right path can be an ego trip that is more about pride or achievement than about deepening our life in Christ.

Second, in the parable of the Pharisee and the tax collector, Jesus reminds us to rely more on God's mercy than on our own efforts or accomplishments (Lk 18:9–14). The Pharisee counts his achievements over sin as blessings from God—at first glance a praiseworthy attitude—but in reality, he is focusing on himself and his own achievements, on being "better than." The tax collector, instead, is aware of his sinfulness and prays to God for mercy. The

Pharisee has closed himself off from further growth, in contrast to the tax collector who begs God to step into his life.

Humble awareness of our need for God makes us receptive to God's grace. In the broken bread of the Eucharist, Jesus delights in offering us grace in surprising places—even in our struggles with our sinfulness.

Bread for the hungry

Although we don't always acknowledge it, we come to every Eucharistic Celebration soul-hungry. We hunger for inner peace, meaning, connection, unconditional love, freedom from the slavery of sin. In the Eucharist, Jesus is the *Ultimate Source* of peace, meaning, unity, love, and happiness. Jesus strengthens our individual identity and nurtures our feeble efforts at good works into virtue. As we become more of who we are—*our best selves*—we share ourselves and our love with others.

Bread for the broken

One of the gifts of the Eucharist that is often overlooked is healing. Just as a wholesome life of healthy food, rest, and exercise can heal us physically, the healing love of Jesus can quite literally make us whole from the bitterness of sufferings, injury, or grief. Sins of grave and cruel injustice such as persecution, abuse, enslavement, and torture haunt not only the sinner but also the persons sinned against. For those wounded by this kind of horror, the healing love of Jesus in the Eucharist can become a sanctuary. As the memorial of His unjust persecution and death, the broken Bread of Life has a special power to heal those who have suffered so unjustly.

As the actual presence of Jesus Risen among us, the Eucharist is especially effective in overcoming the lingering effects of any injustice or wounds that we have suffered, so that they no longer hold destructive power over us.

Bread for the fragmented

Gathered around the gift of the Eucharist, we share in the one Bread and the one Chalice that have become Christ. At the Last Supper, Jesus could have chosen many elements from the Passover meal. He chose the simple, almost universal symbols of bread and wine. Sharing a meal shapes our understanding of the Eucharist as the sacrament of unity.

At a family meal, everyone gathers around the table with a certain equality. Everyone has a place, shares the same food, comes at the same time to receive nourishment together. At a meal, we let down our guard and share our vulnerabilities as human beings: our need for food, companionship, and family.

The Eucharist *makes* the Church what it is: we share not just the Sacred Banquet where Christ becomes present in the consecrated Bread and Wine of the Eucharist, but also the Memorial of the sacrifice of His life for us. Our shared Memorial becomes a time of shared purpose: of thanksgiving, adoration, self-offering. Each Eucharistic encounter is an invitation for us individually and communally to grow in union with God and in love for one another, especially the poorest among us.*

---

* You may use this second part of the chapter to make an hour of adoration by praying with the additional suggestions set apart in the boxes, or you can simply continue reading.

In the Light of God's Word

Theme for Holy Hour:

The Power of Christ's Eucharistic Love

Who will separate us from the love of Christ? Will hardship, or distress, or persecution, or famine, or nakedness, or peril, or sword? As it is written,

> "For your sake we are being killed all day long;
> we are accounted as sheep to be slaughtered."

No, in all these things we are more than conquerors through him who loved us. For I am convinced that neither death, nor life, nor angels, nor rulers, nor things present, nor things to come, nor powers, nor height, nor depth, nor anything else in all creation, will be able to separate us from the love of God in Christ Jesus our Lord (Rom 8:35–39).

Suggested opening hymn: "Love Divine, All Loves Excelling," written by Charles Wesley and adapted by C.T. Andrews.

Begin with a personal act of thanksgiving for God's saving love in your life.

Adoring Jesus in His Word

According to these profoundly consoling words of Saint Paul, we have nothing to fear because *nothing* can separate us from God's love. Even the power of sin is subject to God's love, because Jesus died to save us both from our sins and from the

Would you like to make this passage from Romans the bedrock of your spiritual journey? What other passage can inspire you on your daily journey to holiness?

effects of sin. Saint Paul explains that this is how we know that we are loved: "But God proves his love for us in that while we still were sinners Christ died for us" (Rom 5:8).

Romans 8 could become the bedrock of our spiritual lives, because it helps us to focus our beliefs and our trust exactly where they belong: in God. For Saint Paul, the love of Christ transforms his view of life so that even the most difficult or destructive of life's circumstances are not the last word; Christ's love is.

For many people, this passage is quite consoling. But I remember a time in my life when I resisted this passage: it didn't seem to touch me at all. I thought that it had more to do with Saint Paul's fervor than the love of God. "Of course Saint Paul couldn't be separated from God's love—he was a saint!"

As you reflect on this reading, what is the last word for you in the difficulties that you face right now? Express your faith in God by praying this passage again as an act of faith: I believe that nothing can separate me from the love of Christ. . . .

Following Jesus Way

One day when I was given this passage to pray with *again*, I unexpectedly realized that we have it on record that Saint Paul actually struggled with the very challenges he lists here, except for famine. (Saint Paul certainly suffered from hunger during his travels, but I don't remember any Scriptural reference to Saint Paul suffering from a famine.) He really knows what he is talking about because he underwent all of them: *hardship, distress, persecution, nakedness, peril, sword.* And I wondered if I wrote down a list of the challenges that I've faced, which would come out on top—God's love or my struggles?

My list of challenges was certainly not as dramatic as Saint Paul's, but it was real. I brought my list to my hour of adoration, and I suddenly realized that God's love *could* reach past all of my problems; it was just that I often didn't recognize how God was working in my problems, or around them, or in some surprising cases, through them.

Ever since then, I have asked God to allow the reality and power of His love for me to *soak in*. Jesus in the Eucharist has become for me the most dramatic proof of the ever faithful, indestructible, embracing love of God who conquers every problem, every difficulty, and every challenge—not by making them disappear, but by transforming them into opportunities for me to grow in my love for the One who gave His life for me.

> In the presence of Jesus, make a list of all the challenges that you have faced or are facing right now. Present your list to Jesus, asking for the light to see how He is working in your life within these very challenges.

Blessed James Alberione offers his insight into the life of someone whose vision has been transformed by love:

"When [a soul perfected in love] contemplates the Host and Jesus who immolates Himself on the altar, she feels like a drop lost in the ocean of love. 'She sees all in One; she loves all in One.' When she contemplates nature—the sea, the mountains, flowers, fruits—she does not contemplate them for their own sake, but sees in them God the Creator, who made everything out of love. She raises herself from material things to God. God is always present and forms one thing alone with her. 'It is God who offers me this delight now; it is God who permits this affliction for me.'"[1]

> Pause to reflect on how your faith and trust in Christ's love affect how you face the sufferings and obstacles of your life.

How has Christ's love transformed my joys and sufferings? When I've undergone experiences of death and resurrection in my life, how has God been present?

Living in the embrace of God's love is a mystery that may not always make sense on a human level; sometimes a life of union with Christ goes beyond our human understanding into the realm of faith, hope, and love.

Express in your own words both your sorrow for when you did not act out of faith and love, and your desire to let Christ's love rule your mind, heart, and actions by praying, "Lamb of God. . . ."

In Union with Jesus

PRAYER

I pray that, according to the riches of his glory, he may grant that you may be strengthened in your inner being with power through his Spirit, and that Christ may dwell in your hearts through faith, as you are being rooted and grounded in love. I pray that you may have the power to comprehend, with all the saints, what is the breadth and length and height and depth, and to know the love of Christ that surpasses knowledge, so that you may be filled with all the fullness of God.

Ask for the grace to become a person transformed by Christ's love by praying this powerful prayer of Saint Paul.

After you have finished praying this prayer for yourself, pick someone with whom you struggle to get along, and pray this prayer for them, too—that Christ's love may transform his or her life. Finally, pray this prayer a third time for a community that you belong to that needs the transforming power of Christ's

Now to him who by the power at work within us is able to accomplish abundantly far more than all we can ask or imagine, to him be glory in the church and in Christ Jesus to all generations, forever and ever. Amen (Eph 3:16–21).

love—e.g., your family, your parish, your prayer group, or group of volunteers. Suggested hymn to close your adoration: the traditional chant, "Ubi Caritas," or "God Is Love," written by Timothy Reeves.

⚜ Chapter 10 ⚜

From the malignant enemy, defend me

These last couple of petitions of the *Anima Christi* prayer remind us of the vigilance we need on our journey to transformation in Christ. This petition acknowledges our powerlessness to live the fullness of the Christian life on our own. We plead for Christ's protection from the devil, from the terrible evils of our day, from our own tendencies to sin, and from whatever can lead us into sin.

"From the malignant enemy"

Today, people often think about the devil from one of two popular mindsets, neither of which is helpful in the spiritual life:

1. The materialistic denial or dismissal of the devil's very existence and power is spiritually dangerous because it deters vigilance and makes it easier for the devil to act without

being recognized. The horrific evils present in our world today challenge materialism's denial of all that is spiritual. In *The Screwtape Letters*—the fictional account of a junior devil being taught the "art" of temptation by a senior devil—C. S. Lewis compellingly describes how the devil studies our weaknesses to exploit us precisely in those areas where we are prone to fall.

2. An exaggerated, superstitious regard for the power of the devil narrows one's approach to life into attitudes of fear and defensiveness. A view of the world that sees the devil everywhere denies God's omnipotence and the goodness of God's creation. This weakening of faith can foster rigidity, isolation, a judgmental attitude, and a lack of tolerance that can lead to treating others without respect or compassion.

Neither denial of the devil's existence nor exaggerating the devil's power is spiritually helpful. Instead, the Church encourages vigilance, frequent prayer, and faith. "Discipline yourselves, keep alert. Like a roaring lion your adversary the devil prowls around, looking for someone to devour" (I Pt 5:8).

As vigilant as we must be against the devil, we must also be vigilant against our own sinful tendencies, and anything or anyone that would lead us into sin. Self-knowledge is critical so that we can be vigilant. For example, to which of the seven capital sins are we most prone? We become our own enemy when we put ourselves into occasions where it would be easy to sin, or into situations in which we have sinned before. Other people can lead us into sin by their acts of violence, bad example, or persuasion to act against Gospel values.

Yet, since everyone is loved into being by God, even when someone's words or actions become an occasion of sin or suffering for us, the person is not truly our enemy. On the contrary, sometimes he or she is one of the very people we are called to evangelize, with a firmness of purpose, an uncompromising witness, and a tireless, patient response. While Jesus gives us the example of taking a stand against injustice and always giving primacy to God, He also asks us to love our enemies and to do good to those who harm us. Jesus called no one *His* enemy while He was on earth. He calls us to live in an attitude of forgiveness that transforms enemies into brothers and sisters.

Many of the saints, such as Stephen, Thomas More, Rita, and Maria Goretti, give us inspiring and challenging examples of how, with the grace of God, we can combat evil and yet forgive evildoers. Saint Cristóbal Magallanes was a priest in Mexico during the violent persecution of the government against the Catholic Church. Father Cristóbal resisted the unjust oppression for decades; he continued his priestly ministry despite threats and persecution and even started several seminaries, which the government closed down. He also preached against armed rebellion. Finally, he was arrested while on the way to celebrate Mass. Executed four days later, in his last moments he not only proclaimed his innocence, but also forgave those responsible for his death. Father Cristóbal spent his last breath asking God to use his death to bring about peace for his country.

" . . . defend me"

How does the Lord defend us against "the enemy" all around us—the devil, the temptations of the world, and the inconstancy of our own hearts? *By loving us.*

The sheltering love of the Lord is often referred to in the psalms (see Ps 27, 91, 103, etc.). The Lord's saving sacrifice of love—made present to us anew each day in the Eucharistic Celebration—is more powerful than any evil or temptation.

Our own weakness is what makes us most vulnerable to sin, to temptation, to the devil. God's love is our best defense. When we know and trust that we are embraced by His love, we are freed from our ego's demands, from the power of the devil's temptations, from the seduction of the worldly, selfish, materialistic, and overindulgent. Love frees us to make our own choices and to become our best selves, unconstrained by fear, hatred, neediness, envy, loneliness, etc.

Jesus became defenseless for us. He took on all the consequences of evil for love of us. In His death on the cross, Christ robbed evil of its ultimate power and brought the power of His resurrection into even the most destructive of situations.

It is a divine paradox: the defenseless posture of Jesus on the cross makes His loving embrace of us unassailable. This paradox—that in weakness God reveals His power—is magnified in the Eucharist. In the humility of the Eucharist, we behold how Jesus becomes weak—a frail wafer of bread—to give us strength. Personally witnessing the humility of Jesus in the Eucharist can comfort and strengthen us when we feel weak or tempted.

In moments of temptation or spiritual darkness, we may feel God has abandoned us. This is exactly what the devil wants. Discouragement weakens our resolve, and the devil will try to take advantage of that weakness. If instead we take refuge in Christ's love, we open ourselves to the grace to remain faithful amid temptation.*

---

* You may use this second part of the chapter to make an hour of adoration by praying with the additional suggestions set apart in the boxes, or you can simply continue reading.

In the Light of God's Word

Theme for Holy Hour:

Christ's Sheltering Love

Then they seized him [Jesus] and led him away, bringing him into the high priest's house. But Peter was following at a distance. When they had kindled a fire in the middle of the courtyard and sat down together, Peter sat among them. Then a servant-girl, seeing him in the firelight, stared at him and said, "This man also was with him." But he denied it, saying, "Woman, I do not know him." A little later someone else, on seeing him, said, "You also are one of them." But Peter said, "Man, I am not!" Then about an hour later still another kept insisting, "Surely this man also was with him; for he is a Galilean." But Peter said, "Man, I do not know what you are talking about!" At that moment, while he was still speaking, the cock crowed. The Lord turned and looked at Peter. Then Peter remembered the word of the Lord, how he had said to him, "Before the cock crows today, you will deny me three times." And he went out and wept bitterly (Lk 22:54–62).

Suggested opening hymn: "There's a Wideness in God's Mercy," by Frederick W. Faber, or "Hold Me in Life," written by Huub Oosterhuis and translated by David Smith and Forrest Ingram (based on Psalm 25).

As you begin your adoration, pray to the Holy Spirit to help you discern the loving action of God in your life.

Adoring Jesus in His Word

Perhaps our first response to this reading is the question: Why—and how—could Peter betray the Lord just hours after he so strongly declared his loyalty? But then we quickly realize that our question is not so much about Peter but about ourselves. How many times have we declared our love for the Lord and resolved to imitate Him more faithfully, only to find ourselves in even greater need of forgiveness?

The inconstancy of our behavior and of our own hearts rightly haunts us, but when we examine our thoughts, choices, and motivations, we need to do so under the *compassionate gaze of Jesus.*

The real question in this Gospel is: Why would Jesus turn to look at Peter just after he denied Him a third time?

Throughout the Gospels, Jesus never blames anyone for hurting Him. He speaks and defends the truth unapologetically but never defends His own person. Even when Judas betrays Jesus, His reproach is not blame, but more of a warning for Judas.

Jesus gazing on Peter at that moment has one purpose only—to communicate His love and compassion in the very midst of Peter's haunting betrayal. The love of Jesus is faithful—stronger than any evil, even our sins and betrayals. That gaze seared Peter to the heart. It would also sustain him through the darkness of the crucifixion and death of his Master—and perhaps through the rest of his life.

So many people picture God as a wrathful Judge who looks on us in contempt when we sin. Instead, our loving Father looks on us with compassion, regretting the harm that our sinfulness causes—not just to others, but also to us. At the moment that Peter betrayed Jesus out of fear and weakness, Jesus took that weakness on Himself and transformed it. Both Peter's denial and Christ's forgiving gaze marked Peter for the rest of his life. The leader of the Church would be a man forever humbled by his own weakness *and* forever strengthened by his experience of the absolute fidelity of Christ.

What a marvelous grace to pray for: to be transformed by the mercy of Christ!

Let us read again the passage from Luke 22, imagining that we are

> Pray Psalm 18 in gratitude for the sheltering love and mercy of God present and active in your own life.

present at that time and place.
Perhaps we stand in Peter's sandals
and are stunned by the compassion

Following Jesus Way

in Jesus's eyes. Perhaps we are a bystander who is deeply moved by
the loving gaze of Jesus. Perhaps we are one of the servants puzzling
over Peter's tears.

After we prayerfully enter this scene, let us put ourselves in the
place of Peter and openly bring Jesus our sins:

What sin is deeply rooted in me, the most humiliating sinfulness that I struggle with? Can I bring this to Jesus now? How does
Jesus respond with His saving love—a gaze of gentle compassion?
the healing touch of His hand?

The Almighty God who knows the number of the stars also
knows our hearts better than we do. He knows our weakness . . . and
He also knows our muddled desires for goodness, for union with
Him. As we surrender our sinfulness to His loving mercy, we lay it
at His nail-pierced feet. *This* is why He died for us—so that sin can
no longer claim any power over us.

We allow Christ's loving gaze to warm us, embrace us, and shel-
ter us. Though we may fail and fall into sin again, we allow His love
to lift us up in hope—that His love, grace, and mercy will triumph
in the end. Jesus did not just die for us, He also rose for love of us;
and we share not only in His death, but also in His resurrection.

Our struggle with sin is fittingly seen as spiritual battle, with
eternal consequences. A *going into battle* mentality highlights various
helpful attitudes to bring into our spiritual lives, such as vigilance,

single-mindedness, determination, discipline, and self-denial. Our primary weapon—both defensive and offensive—is our relationship with God. Saint Paul encourages us:

"Finally, be strong in the Lord and in the strength of his power. Put on the whole armor of God, so that you may be able to stand against the wiles of the devil. For our struggle is not against enemies of blood and flesh, but against the rulers, against the authorities, against the cosmic powers of this present darkness, against the spiritual forces of evil in the heavenly places. Therefore take up the whole armor of God, so that you may be able to withstand on that evil day, and having done everything, to stand firm. Stand therefore, and fasten the belt of truth around your waist, and put on the breastplate of righteousness. As shoes for your feet put on whatever will make you ready to proclaim the gospel of peace. With all of these, take the shield of faith, with which you will be able to quench all the flaming arrows of the evil one. Take the helmet of salvation, and the sword of the Spirit, which is the word of God" (Eph 6:10–17).

> You may wish to pray with these words of Ephesians, asking Jesus to shelter and strengthen you.

Ephesians 6 gives us an entire arsenal of spiritual weapons, but specifically mentions the word of God as the "sword of the Spirit" which can free us from every evil, every trap, every deception. Many conversions—including Saint Augustine's—were precipitated by reading the word of God. Blessed James Alberione believed so much in the power of God's word that he

> Make a list of favorite Scripture passages to turn to whenever you are overwhelmed, discouraged, or feel the pull of temptation or weakness. Pray with one of them now.

wanted every member of his religious family to carry a passage of the Gospel on his or her person.

Out of their personal experience, many of the saints emphatically recommend turning to Mary the Mother of Jesus as the sure way to

In Union with Jesus through Mary

grow in union with Christ. Blessed James Alberione wrote: "Mary participates in the Eucharistic mission of the Divine Master. In Mass, Communion, and Eucharistic visits we always find Jesus, the Son of Mary. The application of the merits of Jesus Christ, from Calvary to the completion of the centuries, is made by Mary. At the crib, in the temple of Jerusalem, at Cana, Mary is always there. . . . Usually she followed Jesus when He preached, and on Calvary she participated in His sorrows. In her heart and her arms she carried the growing Church which today she defends, comforts, and sustains."[1]

When Jesus entrusted Mary to us as our Mother, He gave us one of the greatest treasures we could ask for on our journey to union with Him.

Prayer to the Queen of Apostles

I thank you, merciful Jesus, for having given us Mary as our Mother. And I thank you, Mary, for having given the Divine Master, Jesus, Way and Truth and Life, to the world, and for having accepted us all as your children on Calvary.

Your mission is united to that of Jesus, who "came to seek those who were lost." Therefore, oppressed by my sins, faults, and negligence, I take refuge in you, Mother, as my supreme hope. Turn your eyes of mercy toward me. Bestow your most maternal care upon me, your neediest child.

I place all my trust in you for pardon, conversion, and sanctity. Form a new class among your children, that of the neediest: those in whom sin has taken root, where formerly abounded grace. This will be the class that will most move you to pity. Receive my poor soul into this class. Work a great wonder by changing this great sinner into an apostle. It will be an unheard-of wonder and a new glory for your Son Jesus and for you, His and my Mother.

Pray the Rosary, asking Mary to help you especially where you feel most vulnerable. Entrust your vulnerability and struggles to her, knowing that she will draw you closer to her Son.

To conclude this time of adoration, sing a hymn to our Blessed Mother, such as the traditional chant, "Hail, Holy Queen," or "Mary, Woman of the Promise," written by Mary Frances Fleischaker.

I hope to receive everything from your heart, Mother, Teacher, and Queen of the Apostles. Amen.[2]

— Blessed James Alberione

❖ Chapter 11 ❖

In the hour of my death, call me and bid me come to You

The final petition, which is so rich it will take two chapters to cover, is a prayer for the last moments of our lives. It reminds us of the eternal purpose for which God created and sustains us.

"In the hour of my death"

Like the Hail Mary, the ending of this prayer focuses on the end of our journey here on earth, the decisive moments when we are about to enter eternity. Our faith can be strengthened when we consider the moment of our death, a practice recommended by many saints—from the Fathers of the Church up to Blessed Teresa of Calcutta. Catholic tradition wisely encourages us to reflect on the "Four Last Things," which refer to death, judgment, heaven, and hell.

The thought of death reminds us how fragile—and thus how precious—is the gift of life. When we remember how short our time is on earth, we are more likely to give priority to what is truly important in our lives.

Every year, all of the sisters of my community make a weeklong retreat. Almost every retreat directs us to meditate on both the shortness and purpose of our lives. These are some of the questions I ask myself:

- ✤ If this were the last year of my life, what would I do differently?
- ✤ Where do I want to be at the end of my life: in my spiritual life, my relationships, my personal growth, my mission?
- ✤ How have I fulfilled the vocation God has entrusted to me?
- ✤ How has my life made a difference to others?
- ✤ How have I used the gifts God has given me?

Time is the way God gives us to grasp the immense gift of our lives. With our gaze fixed on eternity, our heart and feet are planted solidly in the present moment, where God's grace can work in us and through us. We are all called to live this balance between time and eternity not in anxiety but in awareness.

Death unsettles our culture, which often tries to pretend that it does not exist. Yet, one of the few things we can predict with certainty is that someday we will die. As a woman religious, I live in a community with a counter-cultural attitude toward death. I have been privileged to personally witness the last moments of life of several sisters. These sisters have surprised me with their readiness—even their eagerness—to "go beyond." Having lived their entire lives in the light of eternity, at their final moments their faith gives them clearer vision than the rest of us. Death is not an ending but a beginning.

In 1937, Sister Mary Nazarene Prestofilippo was one of the first young women to enter the Daughters of St. Paul, newly founded in the United States. When I first visited the community almost fifty years later, I was struck by Sister Nazarene's vibrant friendliness, her short stature, her lively remarks, and the community's loving nickname for her, "Sister Naz." While I never had the opportunity to become a close friend, she was always a sister with whom I could share a friendly word.

With each passing year, Sister Nazarene's health gradually declined. As her prayer became her work, she generously offered her life for many intentions—especially vocations to priestly and religious life. With her kidneys gradually failing, she underwent dialysis three times a week. I think it was at this point that she started talking more about heaven—she felt ready to go! In the last months of her life, she complained several times, "What is taking Him so long?" Her question was no joke, nor a desire to alleviate suffering. Instead, it was an expression of her deep longing to *finally* be completely united to Christ. Her faith bolstered the sisters who accompanied her in her last days, and her funeral became a celebration of life for all of us.

" . . . call me and bid me come to You"

The moment of death and other critical moments of our lives—such as profound religious experiences—are sacred moments where God most directly touches us. God's final call, "Come to me," which we hear regularly at Mass and Eucharistic adoration, will be irresistible if our entire lives have been a preparation for eternal life with Him. God's call will enable us to make our last choice a complete surrender of ourselves into His hands—an incredibly beautiful way to crown our lives.

If we want our death to be a beautiful offering of ourselves to God, we can begin to prepare ourselves now by

- ✠ giving priority to our relationship with God, learning to listen to His call in our daily life;

- ✠ living in love so that we will be ready for new life in the eternal kingdom of love;

- ✠ learning how to surrender to the Lord in the many "daily deaths," or little detachments that we undergo, so that we can learn how to give ourselves completely to Him.*

In the Light of God's Word

"I am the bread of life. Your ancestors ate the manna in the wilderness, and they died. This is the bread that comes down from heaven, so that one may eat of it and not die. I am the living bread that came down from heaven. Whoever eats of this bread will live forever; and the bread that I will give for the life of the world is my flesh."

Theme for Holy Hour:
Jesus, the Bread of Life

The Jews then disputed among themselves, saying, "How can this man give us his flesh to eat?" So Jesus said to them, "Very truly, I tell you, unless you eat the flesh of the Son of Man and

---

* You may use this second part of the chapter to make an hour of adoration by praying with the additional suggestions set apart in the boxes, or you can simply continue reading.

drink his blood, you have no life in you. Those who eat my flesh and drink my blood have eternal life, and I will raise them up on the last day; for my flesh is true food and my blood is true drink. Those who eat my flesh and drink my blood abide in me, and I in them. Just as the living Father sent me, and I live because of the Father, so whoever eats me will live because of me. This is the bread that came down from heaven, not like that which your ancestors ate, and they died. But the one who eats this bread will live forever." (Jn 6:48–58)

Suggested opening hymn: "O Sacrum Convivium" (traditionally attributed to Saint Thomas Aquinas), or "I Am the Bread of Life," by Suzanne Toolan, RSM (based on John 6).

Adoring Jesus in His Word

These words of Jesus can be especially powerful for those who have had an up-close encounter with death—either personally or through the death of a loved one. Jesus calls Himself "the Bread of Life" and promises eternal life to those of us who partake in the Eucharist. How blessed we are to have this tremendous gift of the Eucharistic Presence of Jesus, a foretaste of His promise to share eternal life with us.

The beautiful prayer attributed to Saint Thomas Aquinas, *O Sacrum Convivium*, praises God for the three ways Jesus unites us to Himself in the Most Blessed Sacrament—in the past, in the present, and in the future.

O Sacred Banquet	*O sacrum convivium*
in which Christ is received,	*in quo Christus sumitur*
the memory of His passion is renewed,	*recolitur memoria passionis eius*

the soul is filled with grace	*mens impletur gratia*
and a pledge of future glory	*et futurae gloriae*
is given us,	*nobis pignus datur,*
Alleluia.	*Alleluia.*

The First Way: Sacred Banquet

Jesus *is* the Sacred Banquet. As the host, He invites us to draw near; then He becomes the meal, feeding us with the "bread" of His word and with His very self in the transubstantiated Bread and Wine which become His Body and Blood.

Jesus holds nothing back, giving Himself so completely to us that the only limit to our union with Him is our own limited capacity. As the Bread of Life, Jesus wants to nourish us spiritually, strengthening our faith, hope, and love so that we can be always more intimately united with the Father through Christ, in the Holy Spirit.

This profound union with Jesus in Communion can sometimes give us tremendous joy; at other times that joy is hidden from us. But whether we feel it or not, every Communion deepens our union with Christ, transforms us further into His image, and strengthens us for our mission of witnessing to the Gospel. Praying the following prayer is one way we can more intentionally unite ourselves with Christ in the Mass.

OFFERING OF THE HOLY MASS

Accept, Most Holy Trinity, this sacrifice fulfilled at one time by the divine Word and now renewed on this altar through the hands of Your priest. I unite myself to the intentions of Jesus Christ, Priest and Lamb of God, that I may be entirely offered for Your glory and for the salvation of all people. Through Jesus Christ, with Jesus Christ, and in Jesus Christ, I intend to adore

> At every Mass, Jesus invites you to enter with Him into the life of the Trinity. Pray this *Offering of the Holy Mass* the next time you go to Mass.

Your eternal majesty, to thank Your immense goodness, to satisfy Your offended justice, and to beseech Your mercy for the Church, for my dear ones, and for myself.

— Traditional, adapted

The Second Way: Sacred Memorial

At the Last Supper, Jesus clearly offers the Eucharist as a memorial of His upcoming passion, death, and resurrection—His self-offering to

> Following Jesus Way

the Father on our behalf. "This is my blood of the covenant, which is poured out for many for the forgiveness of sins" (Mt 26:28).

Even though the Mass is an unbloody offering in the form of bread and wine, the sacrifice of Jesus at every Mass is as complete as it was on Calvary. Every time we go to Mass, Jesus offers Himself for us again. How can we respond?

I. Adore and thank Jesus for the gift of our Redemption. We can thank Him for the merciful love that forgives our sinfulness without a second thought; for the creative love that sustains us in our very existence; for the loving plan to bring us to the joys of heaven.

2. Offer ourselves with Jesus to the Father. United to Christ's adoration, surrender, and thanksgiving to the Father, our offering is especially pleasing to the Father. Eucharistically surrendering our love and our lives with Jesus to the Father, we grow in our love for Jesus, grow into His image, and prepare for an eternity of union with God.

When we think about eternity, Blessed James Alberione encourages us to focus not on our fears but on taking advantage of the great mercy extended to us.

"We might be filled with a certain fear: How will I appear at the judgment seat of God? He had certain plans for me; He gave me natural and supernatural gifts . . . a huge amount of means, graces, and gifts! . . . So then, it comes down to this: let us ask for such an increase of grace, of mercy, and of good will that we will be able to do all that the Lord expects from each of us individually. . . . We must use the days of our life to glorify the Master, to live in Him and enable Him to live in us: 'It is Christ who lives in me.'

"Let us rekindle our faith. In fact, let us arm ourselves with a *new faith*—one that concentrates in a special way on this great question: How can I balance my account [with God]?"[1]

How can I live today according to my deepest priorities, to glorify

> Use these questions to examine your conscience and "reset" your priorities according to your eternal goals.

God with my life? How can I open myself to receive more fully the gift of life that Jesus offers me in the Eucharist—at my next Mass or time of adoration?

The Third Way: Sacred Presence

> In Union with Jesus

In becoming truly present not just spiritually but also physically, the Eucharistic Jesus offers us the tremendous gift of His companionship on our journey. His presence in the Eucharist is not static. His is a loving, active, dynamic presence that works within us, developing our capacity for love and preparing us for heaven. As the Risen Jesus accompanied the disciples who didn't recognize Him on the road to Emmaus, so the Risen Jesus in the Eucharist accompanies us in our daily steps. Whether we

> Take some time to rejoice in the loving presence of the Risen Jesus.

begin our adoration feeling discouraged, fearful, joyful, or indifferent, the Risen Master offers us the light of the word of God, rekindles the fire of love in our hearts, and helps us to redirect our steps to follow His way.

PRAYER TO FULFILL MY MISSION

O my God, I will put myself without reserve into Your hands. . . .

God has created me to do Him some definite service; He has

> With this prayer, ask for the grace to live according to God's eternal, loving purpose for you.

committed some work to me which He has not committed to another. I have my mission—I may never know it in this life, but I shall be told it in the next. Somehow I am necessary for His purposes, as necessary in my place as the archangel is in his. If, indeed, I fail, He can raise another, as He could make the stones the children of Abraham. Yet I have a part in this great work. I am a link in the chain, a bond of connection between persons. He has not created me for nothing. I shall do good, I shall do His work. I shall be an angel of peace, a preacher of truth in my own place, while not intending it, if I do but keep His commandments and serve Him in my calling.

Therefore, I will trust Him, whatever, wherever I am, I can never be thrown away. If I am in sickness, my sickness may serve Him; in perplexity, my perplexity may serve Him; if I am in sorrow, my sorrow may serve Him. My sickness, or perplexity, or sorrow may be necessary causes of some great end, which is quite beyond us. He does nothing in vain. He may prolong my life, He may shorten it. He knows what He is about. He may take away my friends, He may throw me among strangers, He may make me feel desolate, make my spirits sink, hide the future from me—still He knows what He is about.

O Adonai . . . I give myself to You. I trust You wholly. You are wiser than I—more loving to me than I myself. Deign to fulfill Your high purposes in me, whatever they may be—work in and through me. I am born to serve You; to be Yours,

A beautiful hymn to conclude your adoration is: "Take, Lord, Receive," by John Foley, SJ (based on the prayer by Saint Ignatius of Loyola).

to be Your instrument. I ask not to see—I ask not to know—I ask simply to be used. . . .

Complete Your work, O Lord, and as You have loved me from the beginning, so make me love You to the end.[2]

— Blessed John Henry Newman

❖ CHAPTER 12 ❖

That with Your saints I may praise You forever and ever. Amen.

The second part of the final petition of the *Soul of Christ* prayer invites us to ponder the reason for our very being: praising God.

"That with Your saints"

One day when I stayed home from school in bed with a fever, I looked for something to read. I picked up *Fifty-Seven Stories of Saints for Boys and Girls*, written and published by the Daughters of St. Paul. I didn't really like short stories, but I couldn't find anything else to read. I opened the book and started reading . . . .

Late that day—about 500 pages later—I closed the book. (I don't know how I hid from my mother that I wasn't sleeping!) My first all-day spiritual speed-read gave me a whole new perspective on the saints. According to this book, the saints were mostly ordinary people who responded in an extraordinary way to the grace of God.

It highlighted their accessibility, humanness, and diversity, and made me feel that even *I* might be called to holiness. After that, I read everything on the saints I could find. I even imagined meeting these fascinating people and talking with them in heaven.

The saints are living Gospels: fallible human beings who "incarnated" the Gospel. Their prayer and lifestyles are rooted in their own times, places, and cultures—always admirable, sometimes inimitable. Our path to sanctity includes *our* particular circumstances, culture, and time—God's particular will for us. We come to know the saints not to imitate them slavishly in the details of their lives, but to imitate their ardor, faith, and love—especially for seeking and following God's will.

When I was co-authoring the two-volume *Saints Alive!* I discovered that every saint has something to teach us, even those with whom we find it hard to identify. But certain saints will touch us deeply and become both friends and models. As we might call on a wise mentor or an older brother or sister, so we can turn to the saints to inspire us and pray for us.

"I may praise You"

Praise is one of the most important aspects of prayer and yet is often greatly neglected. So many times, our first prayer is one of petition or need. If at times we do not feel like praying, our neediness will often drive us to pray.

It is good to express our dependence on God, to turn to God in our need, and to pray for the needs of others. But it is even better to deliberately choose to begin our prayer with praise, because it shifts our attitude toward God.

True love of God seeks God not for what He gives us but for Who He is. When we pray solely out of our own need, we are living only one important aspect of our relationship with God. It can grow into so much more. What do we want our relationship with God to be? Who does God want to be for us?

Only God can answer that last question, but the Scriptures clearly show that God does not just want to solve our little problems, He wants to fill our lives with overflowing Abundance. He wants to be our Happiness, our Holiness, our Salvation, our Joy, our Healing, our Strength, our Refuge, our Beginning and our End, our daily Bread, the Great Romance of our life, the Fire in our souls, the Meaning of our existence. . . .

When we begin our prayer with praise, we move the focus off of ourselves and on to God. Praying in a spirit of praise inspires us to glorify God with our whole lives and anticipates the way that we will pray in heaven. When we lose ourselves in contemplating the goodness of our Beloved God, we begin to experience the joys of heaven.

" . . . forever and ever"

This last phrase highlights our faith in eternal life and our hope that Christ has prepared a place for us. We might hesitate to think much about heaven—either because it is in the faraway future, or because it is important to focus on building the kingdom of God here and now.

Yet the thought of heaven can

- ✥ be a model for building the earthly kingdom of God;
- ✥ strengthen our faith in times of discouragement or doubt;
- ✥ inspire us to action;
- ✥ comfort us in sorrow and suffering with the thought of eternal joy awaiting us.

Although I've believed in heaven and its eternal joys since childhood, it was sometimes hard for me to imagine the glory of heaven. But after my father died, my desire for heaven became more concrete: I can easily imagine the joy of being reunited with my father.

Jesus encourages us to direct our lives to heaven. In the Gospel of Matthew alone, Jesus uses the word *heaven* or *kingdom of heaven* over sixty times. Often, Jesus refers to heaven when He is describing His Father—the Father in heaven. In John 6, Jesus promises that as the Bread of Life, He will raise us up to share in His risen, eternal life. We are called to live in this joyful Eucharistic hope.

"Amen"

"Amen" is a word borrowed from Hebrew but we Catholics take it for granted, using it as a period to end our prayers. "Amen" has been translated as: "verily," "truly," "so be it," "I believe." But these translations don't seem to capture the fullness of meaning in the Hebrew. According to various scholars, in Hebrew "Amen" means that whatever has just been said is both affirmed and committed to.

There are two times throughout our lives as Catholics that our "Amen" takes on special emphasis. The first is at the end of the Eucharistic Prayer when the priest elevates the host and chalice, and we are invited to offer ourselves with Christ to the Father. The second is our act of faith when we receive Communion. With our "Amen" we carry our prayer and self-offering into our day-to-day life. By saying "Amen" at the end of the *Soul of Christ*, we affirm and commit to the desire of Jesus to sanctify us, transform us, and bring us to eternal life with Him.*

In the Light of God's Word

And from the throne came a voice
   saying,
"Praise our God,
all you his servants,
and all who fear him,
small and great."

Then I heard what seemed to be the voice of a great multitude, like the sound of many waters and like the sound of mighty thunderpeals, crying out,

"Hallelujah!
For the Lord our God
the Almighty reigns.
Let us rejoice and exult
and give him the glory,
for the marriage of the Lamb has come,
and his bride has made herself ready;
to her it has been granted to be clothed
with fine linen, bright and pure"—

Theme for Holy Hour:

Offering Ourselves with Jesus

Suggested opening hymn: "Pan de Vida," by Bob Hurd and Pia Moriarty (based on John 13:1–15, Gal 3:28–29) or "Panis Angelicus" (Bread of Angels), traditionally attributed to Saint Thomas Aquinas, or "See Us, Lord, About Your Altar," written by John Greally.

Adoring Jesus in His Word

---

* You may use this second part of the chapter to make an hour of adoration by praying with the additional suggestions set apart in the boxes, or you can simply continue reading.

for the fine linen is the righteous deeds of the saints.
And the angel said to me, "Write this: Blessed are those who are invited to the marriage supper of the Lamb." And he said to me, "These are true words of God" (Rev 19:5–9).

The Glory of the Mass

Every time we participate at Mass, we have a foretaste of the heavenly banquet described in this reading from the Book of Revelation as the wedding feast of Jesus, the Lamb of God, and His Bride, the Church.

The Eucharist is our *close encounter* with God, our way to holiness. The Eucharist is also "the source and summit of Christian life" (*Lumen Gentium*, no. 11). It unites earth and heaven in praising God. The Eucharistic Celebration is the only perfect prayer of praise because Jesus offers Himself with us: in the Eucharist, all of creation is raised in praise and self-offering to God in Christ.

At the Eucharistic Celebration, we are privileged to celebrate the holiest of mysteries, although much of its glory is hidden under the veil of the words and gestures of the priest and those who are participating. Jesus truly offers Himself at every Mass and is truly present in the Holy Eucharist, but both His sacrifice and presence are hidden from our ordinary sight. In heaven, there will be no veil. We will see Christ face to face; we will finally be truly and fully united with Him.

The Saints and the Mass

The glory of the Eucharist, this great Mystery of Love, is too vast for us to contemplate most of the time. But every once in a great while, the Holy Spirit's breath stirs and briefly lifts up the veil for us, sometimes through the lives of the saints.

Many saints had a particularly strong love for the Eucharist:

- ⚓ Saint Elizabeth Ann Seton was initially attracted to Catholicism because of the Eucharist.

- ⚓ Saint Pio of Pietrelcina (Padre Pio), a stigmatist who participated visibly in Christ's passion, took an hour to prepare for celebrating his daily Mass, which could last up to three hours due to his great reverence, tears, and contemplation.

- ⚓ Saint Clare of Assisi raised the Eucharist above the walls of her convent to protect the sisters against armed invaders. The invaders fled in fear, leaving the convent unharmed.

- ⚓ Saint Paschal Baylon, a simple Franciscan friar of sixteenth-century Spain, risked death to defend the Eucharist before an anti-Catholic mob.

Saints famous for their writings about the Eucharist:

- ⚓ Saint Ignatius of Antioch, Saint Ambrose, Saint Bernard of Clairvaux, Saint Thomas Aquinas, Saint Francis of Assisi, Saint Alphonsus Liguori, Saint Teresa of Avila, Saint Catherine of Siena, Saint Peter Julian Eymard, and Blessed Teresa of Calcutta, among others.

Martyrs of the Eucharist:

- ⚓ Saint Tarcisius, a young man who lived during the early Roman persecutions of the Christians. While bringing Communion to imprisoned Christians awaiting martyrdom, he died protecting the Eucharistic hosts from sacrilege.

⚜ Saint Pedro de Jesús Maldonado, a priest in Mexico who encouraged Eucharistic adoration. Father Pedro was carrying the Eucharist when he was caught by soldiers for violating the government ban on celebrating the sacraments. He was able to consume the Eucharist before he was beaten to death.

These saints can inspire us to reflect on what a great gift the Eucharist has been in our lives.

Blessed James Alberione's writing style is usually spare and direct. But when trying to describe the Mass, he becomes almost poetic. This excerpt is from a meditation he gave:

In your own words, or using the words of the *Gloria*, lovingly praise Jesus in the Eucharist.

Following Jesus Way

"The Mass! Daystar of prayer, queen of devotions, source of the water of life and of the grace which the sacraments communicate!

As you reflect or pray with these words of Blessed James Alberione, in your own words add what you most appreciate about the Mass.

"The Mass! The most effective suffrage for the souls in purgatory!

"The Mass! Light, sacrifice, the grafting of the precious olive into a wild olive—sinful human beings.

"The Mass! The glory of the priest, the strength of martyrs, the nourishment of virgins, the hidden power of apostles, writers, and preachers, and the joy of the true Christian!

"The Mass, celebrated in eternity by the supreme High Priest in heaven, glorifies God and brings joy to the blessed."[1]

——— ❧❧❧ ———

Once when I was struggling with a difficult, deeply painful situation, the Holy Spirit "lifted the veil" of the Eucharist for me. For several months, I had felt as if God had abandoned me. One particular day at Mass, I received the grace to offer more fully the painful situation in union with Christ. Time stopped. It was as if I was standing beneath the cross, offering my life with Jesus.

What startled me wasn't just that I offered myself with Jesus, *but that Jesus was offering Himself with me.* Until then, I hadn't known that one of the greatest sufferings I'd ever undergone could be so intertwined with one of the greatest joys I'd ever know: to be so closely united with Jesus.

> When have you experienced more profoundly the mystery of the Eucharist?

All of us are called to live Eucharistic lives—lives of thanksgiving, praise, and self-offering. How can our prayer become more Eucharistic? How can we live a more Eucharistic life?

> As you reflect on how to live a Eucharistic life, express to Jesus your desire to live in greater union with Him through your participation at Mass.

For the Praise of His Glory

In Union with Jesus

As we increasingly put God at the center of our prayer, hopefully we can also begin to put Him at the center of our lives, as Saint Paul does: "In Christ we have also obtained an inheritance, having been destined according to the purpose of him who accomplishes all things according to his counsel and will, so that we, who were the first to set our hope on Christ, might live for the praise of his glory" (Eph 1:11–12).

To "live for the praise of his glory" means a lot more than beginning our prayer with a hymn of praise. As Saint Paul points out, the praise that God most truly wants is the praise that goes beyond words—the praise of lives dedicated to God. Wholeheartedly offering our lives with Christ in the Eucharistic Celebration is the highest praise that we can give God.

PRAYER
(adapted from Ephesians 1:3–12)[2]

Blessed be You, God and Father of our Lord Jesus Christ, who has blessed us in Christ with every spiritual blessing in the heavens: *May we live for the praise of Your glory!*

> Pray this prayer adapted from the Letter to the Ephesians in the spirit of offering your entire life to the Father, with Christ, in the Holy Spirit.

You, Father, chose us in Christ before the foundation of the world to be holy and blameless before You: *May we live for the praise of Your glory!*

Father, in Your love You destined us beforehand to be Your adopted children through Jesus Christ, according to the purpose and desire of Your will, to the praise of the glorious grace bestowed upon us in Your Beloved: *May we live for the praise of Your glory!*

Through Christ's blood we are redeemed and our sins are forgiven—such is the wealth of Your grace which You poured out upon us! *May we live for the praise of Your glory!*

With every manner of wisdom and understanding You made known to us the mystery of Your will, according to the purpose You displayed in Christ as a plan for the fullness of time—to bring all things together in Christ, things in the heavens and things on earth. *May we live for the praise of Your glory!*

You may wish to conclude your prayer with a spiritual communion using the words of the *Anima Christi* prayer, found on p. ix.

You accomplish all things in accordance with the purpose You have decided upon, and in Christ You chose and selected us in accordance with Your plan by which we who were the first to hope in Christ might exist to praise Your glory. *May we live for the praise of Your glory!*

Close your adoration with a Eucharistic hymn that will remind you to offer not just your prayer but your entire life with Jesus, such as: "Life-Giving Bread, Saving Cup," by James J. Chepponis, or "Bread for the World," by Bernadette Farrell.

❧ APPENDIX ☙

How to Make a Pauline Hour of Adoration

The Pauline Hour of Adoration was developed by Blessed James Alberione, the Founder of the Pauline Family.

Born in 1884 on a poor family farm, James Alberione knew from an early age that he was called to be a priest. Yet his vocational journey was not without struggle. At age sixteen, he was expelled from the minor seminary. Allowed to re-enter the seminary on probation, James received the profound inspiration that would shape his life's work during his all-night Eucharistic vigil on the night of December 31, 1900. Receiving a special light from Jesus in the Eucharist, the young Alberione was deeply moved to do something for the people of his time. Ordained in 1907, Alberione's spiritual and pastoral vision continued to take shape as he became expert in understanding the spiritual needs of the world, which he called "reading the signs of the times." These spiritual needs compelled him to take action. He was inspired to respond to the most urgent needs by founding the ten institutes of the Pauline Family[1]—often in ways ahead of his time and without others' understanding or approval.

Despite poor health and the often excruciating pain that he suffered, Alberione formed the members of the Pauline Family and directed their pastoral initiatives all over the world. Known as one of the most creative apostles of the twentieth century, Alberione died in 1971 and was beatified in 2003, called by Saint John Paul II the "first apostle of the New Evangelization."

For the members of his Pauline Family, Blessed James Alberione mandated a particular way of making Eucharistic adoration—a way that would foster a real personal relationship with Christ, who is our Way, Truth, and Life. The Pauline Hour of Adoration has a simple, three-fold structure dedicated to Jesus our Master and the Truth we believe, Christ the Way we follow, and Jesus our Savior who brings us to the fullness of Life.

Blessed James divides the hour of adoration into three "moments," or parts. In the first part, we adore Jesus, listening attentively to His word to us today and letting his truth shape our minds and attitudes. In the second part, we contemplate Jesus as our Way and Model, and we reflect on our response to His loving presence in our lives. In the third part, we try to open ourselves fully to Jesus our Life, to let His sustaining grace and peace touch and transform our hearts so that we can bring that same peace and love to others.

Guide to Making a Pauline Hour of Adoration

We begin our Eucharistic hour of adoration by becoming attentive to the presence of God. We may need to mindfully slow down, leaving aside the frenetic pace and distractions of our day. We focus our attention on Christ and the gift of this particular time spent in His Eucharistic presence. We may want to ask for a particular grace or offer this hour for a special intention. We open our hearts to the loving appeal of Jesus, "Come to me . . . ." A hymn or prayer of adoration is a good way to enter into a prayerful, attentive spirit. We choose or remind ourselves of the theme of the hour, which can become a recurring motif throughout our prayer.

Adoring Jesus Truth

As we prepare to listen to the word of God, we ask the help of the Holy Spirit to make us receptive.

We read a passage of Scripture, usually chosen ahead of time according to the theme we wish to pray with. (If we don't have time to prepare earlier, we may simply choose a passage as we begin.) We listen attentively and openly. Like young lovers who "hang" on each other's words, straining to hear their beloved's next whisper, we too listen to the word of God with love and trust, knowing that it will not leave us untouched. We let Jesus Truth enlighten us and give us new understanding and insight.

We adore Jesus in His word.

We take the time to re-read the passage; to reflect on it, perhaps conversing with Jesus about how this Scripture passage touches our life and what it means for us today, in our situation. For Blessed James, it is most important to leave time for reflection, allowing the saving word of Jesus to enlighten us, here and now, where we are today.

Adoring Jesus Truth through frequent reading of the Scriptures strengthens our faith and influences our attitudes. We gradually begin to see and experience life more in the light of faith. In fact, faith is a special gift we can ask for during this first part of the hour—a faith that will transform us into better disciples of Jesus.

We conclude this first part by responding to the word of God with an act of faith—an affirmation of our belief in and our commitment to Christ. This act of faith, whether formal or spontaneous, prepares us to follow Jesus more closely.

Following Jesus Way

Having just recommitted ourselves to Christ, in the second part of the hour of adoration we contemplate Jesus as our Way and our Model, and we look more closely at our relationship with Him. Taking up the theme of the Scripture passage and the lights or insights we received, we contemplate God's action in our own lives. (A Jesuit might call this an examen of consciousness, or personal examen.)[2]

First, we reflect on our day, our week, or a certain aspect of our lives and look for the many marvelous ways God has been at work. We thank God for the gifts and blessings given to us, perhaps by praying the Magnificat or another prayer of thanksgiving.

Second, as we become aware of God's many blessings, we realize that we have often failed to respond fully to the graces we have received. We take a few minutes to look more closely at *our* response to God's invitations and gifts, noting our sinfulness. This examination of conscience, which focuses on our response to God, helps us to see how we have sinned and how we need to convert—in our attitudes, thoughts, words, actions, and desires. We confront our lives with Christ's words and example, perhaps even trying to imagine what Jesus would do in our place.

Third, we express our sorrow for our sinfulness and resolve to more faithfully follow Jesus in our life, praying for the grace to live our resolution. As we turn to God with both gratitude and humility, we realize that we do not have the strength to change on our own. But we can renew our trust that God will give us the graces we need to do so. Jesus wants us to trust in Him. He wants us to be His presence in the world today. Through this second part of the hour, we open ourselves to living in continual conversion.

According to Blessed James Alberione, this moment of prayer is important in making our relationship with God "real"—not just contemplating a lofty ideal, nor reserved to private prayer time. Our Eucharistic prayer *is* a relationship that affects every aspect of our lives—our daily struggles, our joys, and our relationships with others. Thanksgiving for God's graces in our lives and realistic knowledge of our daily response to God are both crucial. Without an appreciation of God's goodness to us, we cannot recognize how we have failed to respond to His call. Without recognizing our failures, our thanksgiving might be very superficial. God loves us *in* our weaknesses, not despite them.

In Union with Jesus

Converted anew, we enter the third part of the hour of adoration hungry for greater union with God and more intimate communication with Jesus as our Life, the Source of grace, of strength, and of union with the Father.

United to Christ our Life, we contemplate His love for the Father, for humanity, and for each of us. We become true apostles as we bring to God our own needs and the needs of the world.

Prayers of petition, but also praise and contemplation of God's goodness, rise from our hearts. Whether our prayer is offered spontaneously or more formally in the form of the Rosary, the Stations, the Liturgy of the Hours, a psalm or other prayers, we seek a union of mind, will, and heart with Christ. We offer Jesus our hearts so that we can become completely one with Him and communicate His love to the world.

This is time for "prayer of the heart," that is, letting ourselves be loved by the Lord, sharing with God our needs and our deepest desires, and asking to be transformed into witnesses of His love and truth.

We conclude our hour of adoration with an act of love and return to our daily life refreshed and renewed, recommitted to share Jesus with others.

Practical Notes on Using the Hours of Adoration Individually and for a Group

In general, you will usually find it helpful to bring your Bible and a favorite prayer book. While the Scripture reading is included, other recommended Scriptural passages are only cited. Familiar prayers, such as the Rosary, the Stations, and the Gloria, are recommended but their text is not included.

For Individuals:

These hours of adoration come from the rich tradition of Pauline spirituality and are meant as outlines to guide your Eucharistic adoration. Please use them freely, according to your individual needs and desires, but especially following the lead of the Holy Spirit, the Author of all prayer.

For Groups:

Encourage participants to bring their own Bibles.

- ⚜ Downloadable handouts for each hour—which include only the prayers intended to be prayed aloud together—are available online at: www.pauline.org/mariepaulcurley. They may be printed out for small group use.

- ⚜ When praying these hours of adoration together, allow plenty of time for silence.

- ⚜ Each hour includes suggestions for opening and closing hymns that will resonate with the theme of the holy hour, but these are simply suggestions. Additional hymns will enrich the group's adoration, particularly at the end of each part. The leader will want to choose hymns ahead of time, using an available hymnal.

Adoring Jesus Truth: The Scripture reading is best proclaimed. The leader may wish to ask another participant to read the Scripture passage aloud. The reflection on the reading may be read aloud or silently, if group members have a copy of the book. However, time for silent reflection during this first part should always be provided. At the conclusion, an act of faith may be made together in the form of reciting the Creed or another prayer, singing a hymn, etc.

Following Jesus Way: The leader can guide the group in offering thanks, possibly inviting individuals to share aloud their gratitude to

God. The prayer of thanksgiving can be prayed together, using a hymn or prayer such as the Magnificat.

The examination of conscience may be introduced by the provided quotation or question that sets a direction for personal reflection, but ample silence here is usually the most helpful. The act of contrition and act of trust can be prayed aloud together. An appropriate hymn can help the group renew trust in the Lord and strengthen resolve to follow Jesus more closely.

In Union with Jesus: In the third part, members of the group can be invited to spontaneously express prayer intentions for personal needs and for the needs of the world. The Rosary, the Stations, the Liturgy of the Hours, or individual psalms can easily be prayed together.

Finally, the group may conclude their hour of adoration by singing a hymn that expresses a renewed commitment to living out the Gospel of love in their daily lives.

Notes

Invitation

1. Blessed James Alberione, 1884–1971. Beatified on April 27, 2003. Founder of the Pauline Family and called the "first apostle of the New Evangelization" by Saint John Paul. For more information on his life, read the Appendix, How to Make a Pauline Hour of Adoration one page 145.

Chapter 1

1. Frederick Buechner, *Wishful Thinking: A Seeker's ABC* (San Francisco: HarperSanFrancisco, 1993), 119.

2. John Henry Newman, *Meditations and Devotions*, Part III. Meditations on Christian Doctrine. Hope in God—Creator.

3. James Alberione, *Until Christ Be Formed in You* (Boston: St. Paul Editions, 1983), 11.

4. An explanation of the difference between an examen and the examination of conscience is found in the notes for the Appendix on page 156.

5. *Prayers of the Pauline Family*, printed by the Daughters of St. Paul, 1991. (For Private Use.)

Chapter 2

1. Scott McPherson, *Marvin's Room*, directed by Jerry Zaks [1996; Santa Monica, CA: Miramx Home Entertainment, 1997], DVD.

2. Alberione, *Until Christ Be Formed in You*, 34.

3. Alberione, *That Christ May Live in Me* (Boston: St. Paul Editions, 1980), 39.

4. Alberione, "That I May Love With Your Heart": Thoughts from a personal notebook of Father James Alberione. (Rome: General Historical Archives, 1985), no. 37. (For private use.)

Chapter Three

1. Alberione, *Practices of Piety and Interior Life*, 7 (for private use).

2. *Prayers of the Pauline Family*, 53.

3. *Ibid.*, 55–56.

Chapter Four

1. Alberione, Meditation to the novices in 1956 (for private use).

2. *Prayers of the Pauline Family*, 270.

Chapter Five

1. Delmer Daves and Donald Ogden Stewart, *Love Affair*, produced and directed by Leo McCarey [1939; New York, NY: RKO Radio Pictures, 1998], DVD.

2. Delmer Daves, Leo McCarey, and Donald Ogden Stewart, *An Affair to Remember*, directed by Leo McCarey [1957; Twentieth Century Fox, 2003], DVD.

3. Traditional prayer adapted from: *The Raccolta* or *Collection of Indulgenced Prayers and Good Works*, translated by Ambrose St. John. 1910 edition.

4. Alberione, *Until Christ Be Formed in You*, 52, 55.

5. Traditional prayer adapted from *The Raccolta* or *Collection of Indulgenced Prayers and Good Works*.

Chapter Six

1. *May Christ Arise in Us* (private document of the Daughters of St. Paul, 2011).

2. Alberione, *Practices of Piety and the Interior Life*, 85.

3. Alberione, *Until Christ Be Formed in You*, 60.

4. Alberione, "That I May Love with Your Heart," no. 40.

Chapter Seven

1. Alberione, *Until Christ Be Formed in You*, 56.

2. Alberione, *Practices of Piety and the Interior Life*, 83.

3. Alberione, *Until Christ Be Formed in You*, 55–56.

Chapter Eight

1. Alberione, *Brevi meditazioni per ogni giorno dell'anno,* p. 536, as translated in the *2013 Agenda Paolina* (For private use).

2. *Ibid.,* p. 385.

Chapter Nine

1. Alberione, *Practices of Piety and the Interior Life*, 245.

Chapter Ten

1. Alberione, *Mary, Queen of Apostles* (Boston: St. Paul Editions, 1976), 16.

2. *Prayers of the Pauline Family,* 225–226.

Chapter Eleven

1. Alberione, *Explanation of the Constitutions* (for private use), 333–336.

2. John Henry Newman, *Meditations and Devotions,* Part III, Meditations on Christian Doctrine, Hope in God—Creator.

Chapter Twelve

1. Alberione, *Ut Perfectus Sit Homo Dei: Month of Spiritual Exercises,* April 1960. Second Week, Instruction II, nos. 25–26 (for private use).

2. Adapted from Ephesians 1:3–12, *The New Testament: St. Paul Catholic Edition,* translated by Mark A. Wauck (New York: Society of St. Paul, 2000).

Appendix

1. Every institute of the Pauline Family lives the Pauline spirit—to live and give Jesus Christ Way, Truth, and Life to the world. The Pauline Family is made up of: the Society of St. Paul and the Daughters of St. Paul (priests, religious brothers and sisters who seek to put Christ at the center of culture by using the media to communicate the Gospel); the Disciples of the Divine Master (contemplative sisters who bring the spirit of the Eucharistic liturgy into everyday life); the Sisters of the Good Shepherd (active sisters dedicated to pastoral work in the parish); the Sisters of Mary, Queen of Apostles (sisters who help young people discover and respond to their vocations); the Institute of Jesus the Priest (diocesan priests who find support for their ministry in the vows and the Pauline charism); the Institute of St. Gabriel (secular institute for consecrated single lay men to evangelize in the spirit of St. Paul); Institute of Mary of the Annunciation (secular institute for consecrated single lay women to evangelize in the spirit of St. Paul); the Institute of the Holy Family (secular institute for husbands and wives to revitalize Catholic family life with the Pauline spirit); and the Association of Pauline Cooperators (lay collaborators who live and spread the Gospel in the Pauline spirit).

2. Influenced by Saint Ignatius of Loyola, Blessed James Alberione's understanding of the examination of conscience has similarities to the Ignatian practice of the examen of consciousness. In brief, the examen of consciousness is a practice of discernment. It includes a review of our day, considering God's presence, gifts, and invitations. After recognizing the presence of God, we respond with gratitude and review how we have responded to God's graces. Many Catholics are more familiar with the examination of conscience which is used as a preparation for going to the sacrament of Penance. In this examination, we review our thoughts, words, deeds, desires, and omissions since our last examination of conscience, looking for how we have sinned. The focus is to recognize our sins, ask the Lord's forgiveness, and resolve to change our life. It is a good practice to make the examination of conscience regularly and not just before we go to the sacrament of Reconciliation. Both the examen of consciousness and the examination of conscience are helpful spiritual practices.

Pauline
BOOKS & MEDIA

A mission of the Daughters of St. Paul

As apostles of Jesus Christ, evangelizing today's world:

We are CALLED to holiness
by God's living Word and Eucharist.

We COMMUNICATE the Gospel message
through our lives and through all
available forms of media.

We SERVE the Church
by responding to the hopes and needs
of all people with the Word of God,
in the spirit of St. Paul.

For more information visit our Web site:
www.pauline.org.

BOOKS & MEDIA

The Daughters of St. Paul operate book and media centers at the following addresses. Visit, call or write the one nearest you today, or find us at www.pauline.org.

CALIFORNIA

3908 Sepulveda Blvd, Culver City, CA 90230	310-397-8676
935 Brewster Avenue, Redwood City, CA 94063	650-369-4230
5945 Balboa Avenue, San Diego, CA 92111	858-565-9181

FLORIDA

145 S.W. 107th Avenue, Miami, FL 33174	305-559-6715

HAWAII

1143 Bishop Street, Honolulu, HI 96813	808-521-2731

ILLINOIS

172 North Michigan Avenue, Chicago, IL 60601	312-346-4228

LOUISIANA

4403 Veterans Memorial Blvd, Metairie, LA 70006	504-887-7631

MASSACHUSETTS

885 Providence Hwy, Dedham, MA 02026	781-326-5385

MISSOURI

9804 Watson Road, St. Louis, MO 63126	314-965-3512

NEW YORK

64 W. 38th Street, New York, NY 10018	212-754-1110

SOUTH CAROLINA

243 King Street, Charleston, SC 29401	843-577-0175

TEXAS

Currently no book center; for parish exhibits or outreach evangelization, contact: 210–488–4123 or SanAntonio@paulinemedia.com

VIRGINIA

1025 King Street, Alexandria, VA 22314	703-549-3806

CANADA

3022 Dufferin Street, Toronto, ON M6B 3T5	416-781-9131

¡También somos su fuente para libros,
videos y música en español!